HOW TO KEEP YOUR
X'S & O'S
FROM BECOMING
EXES And WOES

**Yes, You Can Hold Onto & Keep
That New Relationship Sizzle!**

By Cheryl Herbst

With ONLY 3 Daily Practices, You CAN
Empower Yourself & Feel Secure To Love Again!

Published by Legacy Press Books
A subsidiary of S & P Productions, Inc.
311 Main Street, Suite D
El Segundo, CA 90245
310-640-8885
www.legacypressbooks.com

Published and Printed in the United States of America

Cheryl Herbst
13428 Maxella Avenue #253
Marina Del Rey, California 90292
424-226-6112

ISBN 978-1-950326-06-8

DEDICATION

I dedicate this book to my forever soul brother,

Michael D'Angelo.

His decades of loyalty and devotion have given my life the stability and safety that has allowed me to explore it in all its nuances. I know that we have known each other in many facets over many lifetimes, and like Jonathan and Fletcher Seagull, we will know each other forever. Thank you for being my family, my best friend, and my best listener for over 35 years while I figured it out.

WHAT OTHERS SAY

"Outstanding work. It's engaging as well as simple to understand, highly practical and effective. " ~ Mike Begala, Master NLP Trainer

"After reading just the first few pages, I felt empowered and hopeful." ~ Richard Schacter, retired physicist

"It's the cliff notes of relationship strategies. It's very simple. I can see how I could do the work. Made me think." ~ Charlie Trinh, Video Game Designer

"I felt the detail was there so I could implement." ~ Rafael Lopez, Certified Massage Therapist (CMT), BSES

"With what Cheryl offers, nothing can stand in your way from taking action everyday towards having relationships that fulfill you. This is a must-read book if you want to have relationships you love."
~ Dr. Sarah Larsen, Host of Miracle Makers TV

"A succinct and simple recipe book. Cheryl gets me; I felt I wasn't alone. She put me at ease going through a sad situation. I was amazed." ~ Cathy Slade, Sales Consultant

"I absolutely loved this book! So much of what is said in this book is the blunt truth that we have all lived - and lived it emotionally. An awakening! I couldn't wait to turn to the next page to learn more – Could not put this book down. Cheryl Herbst is a talented writer who builds curiosity, wondering what is going to happen next, and then

satisfies that curiosity with learning, completion. Well worth the read – and maybe even a second read!"
~ Jeralyn Sommers, President Private Financial Inc.

"Cheryl knows what she is talking about. She makes sense and gives great examples. Her book has humanity as she shows us how we can be responsible for our own happiness, and choose to be or not. I felt that no matter what, we can make it work." ~ Aaron Matthews, Accounting Coordinator

"Cheryl caught my attention. Very inspiring. Uses minimal words with great meaning. Has great examples. I love the way she hones in on results. It's like she is holding my hand through it. We can fix everything together." ~ George Phillip, President Phillip Solutions

KUDOS TO MY MENTORS

You can't do it wrong, but you can sure do it long. Without mentors, learning takes forever!

Life itself has been an amazing teacher, but it wasn't until I found my mentors that the roadblocks that were keeping me stuck began to break up. I am so grateful, from the depths of my heart, for each one. I encourage everyone to find a coach, a mentor. It's the best way to shorten the path to heaven on earth.

I have also heard it said, *"When the student is ready, the teacher appears."* I have so many to honor, but the tops on my list are:

Dr. Sarah Larsen whose gems of wisdom and insight awakened my spirit from its sleep

Mike Begala whose Life Purpose Mastery program and personal coaching helped me to find my purpose, my identity, and how to bring congruence to all levels of myself, AND whom I consider as my best and favorite role model

Gary Chapman who blessed our world with his book, *The 5 Love Languages*, and educated me on how to make love work

Dr. John Demartini who opens caged minds with his book, *The Heart Of Love*, and educated me on the importance of values in getting my needs met with an unreserved YES

Matt Brauning whose heart-based NLP Mastery program took years off clearing my own self-sabotage and the blocks that kept me from obtaining the pot at the end of my rainbow

Maurice Dimino who got me to believe that practice makes progress, and that my message is inside of me – and needs to come out

Craig Duswalt who taught me that thinking outside of the box is fun, easy and rewarding

And most of all, **Sage Lee,** my branding coach, who helped me to transform teaching into a work of heart

I am deeply appreciative that when I was ready, these awesome mentors and teachers appeared.

I hope, through this book, I become one of yours!

TABLE OF CONTENTS

INTRODUCTION

Are you at the end of a painful breakup, feeling broken, hurt, maybe wondering, "Why can't I make this relationship thing work? Can love really last a lifetime? Why does it have to be so hard?"

Or are you alone – again – maybe even more in love with your memories of that person on the other side of your bed than the actual person sleeping there?

Or do you feel hopeless, wondering, "Where did that sizzle go? Is it possible to reignite the love we once felt?"

How would you like to keep love glowing long after the honeymoon stage is over? Well, I've spent years figuring this out, and I have finally uncovered just 3 ROOT causes that underlie relationship failures. Just 3! Therefore, with just 3 best practices that solve just 3 causes, it's possible to keep your partner wanting to come home to you for decades to come! That's really good news!

Whether you are avoiding, searching, or in a relationship, I want to share with you the 3 BEST practices for simplifying your struggles and eliminating your heartaches. I too had to struggle with such losses. After one, very serious failure, my grief almost took my life! Such grief can put the breaks on trusting yourself to step out there to try again. So what I think is key, is a way to feel SAFE before opening up and attempting love again. To be safe, YOU have to be in charge of the result, not a victim. This book will show you how just 3 daily practices can put YOU in charge so you can CREATE the relationship you have so longed for.

Finally, it's not rocket science! You simply were not taught what YOU were doing that was exhausting your failed

relationships. But when you know better, you do better, right!
YOU become the manager, not the victim. As the manager, you
have the control to diminish the risk of failure and create
certainty. And when the risk is low, you can feel safe that your
x's & o's will never again become exes and woes!

Welcome to How To Keep Your X's & O's from Becoming
Exes & Woes. My name is Cheryl Herbst, and I thank you for
purchasing this little book. I know you have many options, so I
promise this book to be simple, practical, and a good investment
in YOU!

WHAT YOU NEED TO
KNOW FIRST

CHAPTER 1
CAN VULNERABILITY BE SAFE?

The first thing I noticed when Sam and Jane brought me their troubles in our first coaching session was that they didn't even look at each other. When I asked how long they had been together, 10 years was the answer. "Tell me about your first meeting," I queried. What I heard was how much in love they used to be, and how hot they used to think each other was. It was the same story I had heard a thousand times before – the promise of happily ever after, and the disappointment of hopes dashed.

Do you have a similar story of lost love in your life? You're not alone. Do you know that the divorce rate is over 50%? And if you add in all the separations that are not even classified as divorce, can you imagine what the true percentage is of failed relationships?

I've been there too. I know how scary or how lonely or how disappointing relationships can be. By all outward standards, I've been quite a successful person. For 30 years, I was a Senior Vice President of Finance making a couple hundred thousand a year, and living what looked like a really good life. On a professional level, I was well respected. It seems like I was daily coaching my employees with their relationship issues. But in my personal life, success was something I always had to work really hard to gain.

Living in a family that didn't get me, I spent my preteen years in my room, isolated, alone, unable to communicate in a way that made me feel like I was a part of the family. In my high school years, I would gain a few friends – and then lose them as they moved out of my transient home town of Las Vegas, where I grew up. In my dating years, my relationships would start out all excited – and then, eventually erode into apathy or anger and then separation. So relationships were always a struggle for me.

Then one day, after a very disappointing relationship breakup, I had finally had it. I was sitting in my car, in the parking lot of my job, and I was incapable of turning the faucet of tears off. I was breaking down. I was out of control. The tears were so uncontrollable, that I had to call the CFO, my boss, and tell him I was stuck in my car, unable to get to my desk. I was an executive manager, so can you imagine how embarrassing that was to admit I couldn't even manage myself!

This particular heartache went on for almost 2 years. Thank God I had the good will I did at my job. Because I could sit for periods of time on many a day and just stare at this one particular picture on the wall. The picture was of a man in a suit, in an alleyway that was strewn with thrown-away objects. Coming from the top of the canvas, there was this rope (like the kind you see dangling in a gym). And this man was looking up at it. Along the alleyway behind him was a brick building with a pitch-black archway. What I would do is sit in this chair -- staring at that rope --and staring at that dark archway – pondering -- whether I would choose to go up the rope or down into the darkness.

I did break down many a time and tearfully cry, "There's no way that I belong here. How can I go on being a victim in a world of relationships that I have no control over?"

This pain was so excruciating, that at one point, I was even able to convince my best friend, that if I got my affairs in order, I could pick an exit date. Can you imagine your best friend feeling so sorry for you that they're actually willing to help you end your pain?

Obviously I survived that crisis. But surviving it was like clawing my way up a 45-degree mountain to feel better. When I did come out on the other side of my despair, though, I knew -- there just had to be a better way than just hoping to stumble across a perfect partner! And I had to find it, not only for me, but for everyone who needed to end this cycle of pain. And that's why I determined to find an answer – an answer that would solve relationship failure -- once and for all.

Although I had waited and hoped, Prince Charming had never rescued me from my tower of loneliness. And as for soul mates, how many more of those was I going to suffer through before I wised up? No, there had to be a better way. Waiting for that right person to come along who would love me everlasting just wasn't working. And as far I could see, it wasn't working for hardly anyone else either.

So I began to think, *"If I were going to stay on planet earth, then relationships were inevitable. And if I were going to survive life by putting my heart in the freezer, then I might as well have chosen that exit path."* I knew I had to be vulnerable to have a long-term love with another human being, and still my vulnerability was most certain that I was NOT going to risk putting my feelings through that kind of pain again! NO way!

So on one side, my shaky vulnerability insisted on being isolated, or at least protective. But my heart, on the other hand, wanted to be free and open and love. They both had good intentions for my life, so what was I to do?

My vulnerability seemed to be the one winning. Sometimes it protected my heart by pulling back and retreating into a cave of its own little world. At other times, its tactic was to collapse and accept the hopelessness of it all. Sometimes it would try disconnecting so nobody was home to feel anything. At other times, it would demand rigid rules on how relationships had to work. And sometimes, it would lash out at others with a demand to be treated better.

Despite all that, my heart understood the loving protection my vulnerability was attempting to show it, that all these reactions were just defense mechanisms used to keep it safe. My vulnerability's intentions were good, but its results were isolation and loneliness. And so my heart was safely protected by my vulnerability's defenses, but it wasn't happy; it wasn't fulfilled.

"How sad!" I thought. Was I going to live in fear of relationships because my only option was to hope I could stumble upon that right person? Even if I did manage to find another relationship that felt right, was I going to live in fear of its impending doom a few years down the road? But what other choices did I have? It seemed I had to either be closed off and SAFE from pain or be openly vulnerable and FEAR pain.

This conflict between my heart and my vulnerability, however, was too much for me. And so I started to think *"What if they're both wrong? What if those limiting choices were just old handed-down thoughts that I was just assuming to be true?*

What if there WAS a way to be safe AND vulnerable!!!"

CHAPTER 2
WHAT'S THE REAL SOLUTION?

How many times have I limited myself because I ASSUMED something to be true? Why not try a different approach this time? What if there WAS a way to be safe AND vulnerable! This out-of-the-box thought stimulated a renewed surge of hope in me, and I leaped into the research.

But oh my, as soon as I entered my search criteria online, I encountered an *overwhelming* amount of data on relationship strategies. How was I ever going to sift through all that data to figure out which ideas were going to work for me? I didn't want to have to die and live another life before I finished consuming and practicing each technique until I found the right ones! No. Mining the internet for the golden wisdom that was going to work for my situation was simply too time consuming and too complicated. I needed something with more certainty, something I could count on to work for ANYONE. I didn't want to waste any more time on trial and error.

"Anyway," I thought, "wasn't the advice on the internet mostly telling me, in one form or another, to play nice, be considerate, and not shut down communication? I mean, truly, didn't I already know that? And yet my relationships still withered on the vine?"

There had to be a SIMPLER way!

To simplify, for each problem, I began asking myself why it was a problem. By using this process, I was able to peel back its layers until I could see the unfertile soil that was allowing it to exist. Slowly, it began to dawn on me that my *"problems"* weren't really *"problems"* at all! They were merely the

7

weeds growing out of deeper, more root-level causes.

These weeds were my *symptoms*, not my problems.

It was the POOR SOIL that was my actual problem.

I had been focusing on my outward symptoms, and I had continuously failed to produce results. Pulling out a weed here and there had never created the healthy soil for my relationship garden to grow in. However, common sense now pointed out that if I spent my efforts on the ROOT causes, wouldn't I have less weeds to work on?

Wouldn't the weeds AUTOMATICALLY DISAPPEAR!

When I started focusing on the soil that all my relationship weeds were growing in, it was the difference that made the difference. As I began to trace back my own underlying causes, I also studied other relationships in real life and in the media to see how it applied to everyone. I was only interested in finding conclusions that worked for ANYONE, so I knew I wouldn't be wasting any more of my time.

I eventually traced all weeds back to JUST THREE missing nutrients:
1) not feeling loved enough
2) not getting needs met with a happy smile
3) and not being able to openly resolve conflicts.
How much SIMPLER was that going to be to solve! And now, how OVER complicated did all those online strategies of 5 to 50 tips look! There were truly only 3 solutions that I needed.

As I continued to study relationships all around me, I heard example after example of people stumbling through their problems with their partners, blaming and justifying, pouting and whining, guilting, and exerting excessive control or anger – all with a desire to feel more wanted. I constantly asked myself how feeling really loved, how getting their needs met with a smile and how understanding what was behind the curtain of their arguments could have changed how they handled their problems – and thus their results.

What was obvious in these examples was that people did not handle their problems in this way because they wanted to be mean or manipulative. No, it was a simple lack of understanding. They didn't understand how the words they used to communicate their desires were causing the unpleasant feedback they were getting. They were the ones speaking their desire for more love, for getting their needs met, and for being understood. But they were doing it in such a way that

it was creating resistance.

When they did not like the inevitable feedback, they got hurt, sad or afraid, and then acted out with more words that didn't work. This, in turn, perpetuated the loop that was exhausting them.

And yet, there was an upside to this realization:

**If we are doing this to ourselves, then
we could STOP and make another choice!**

We could practice ways of communicating our desire for love, for having our needs met, and for being heard and seen that could keep resistance down and the channels of communication open!!

Don't believe me? Are you insisting that it's still all on your listener? Well, let's try a little experiment. Try setting aside your usual viewpoint, and have a go at this exercise:

- Take notice and pay closer attention to conversations with your friends, lovers or in the media.

- Ask these questions, *"How is the desire for connection and needs being presented? How is it being reacted to? What is each person hearing? What are the dynamics going on behind the scenes of the person speaking?"*

As I did this exercise, on my own conversations, I began to notice comments I would have ignored or refuted in the past. For example, one day my girlfriend had responded to a whining question I had asked with, *"That sounds so manipulative to me."* My typical reaction would have been to get my feelings hurt, and then blamed her for not hearing me. However, with this new viewpoint in mind, I questioned myself instead and said, *"Hmmm. Is it?"* And guess what the honest answer was? *"YES!"* I had never noticed the manipulation in my whining before. Now it was so obviously clear to me, I couldn't see how I managed to have missed it before.

By becoming conscious of what was behind my words, over time, I was able to stop my manipulating. When I finally was able to stop, and learned to make a request with better languaging instead, I was surprised at how willing people were to help me, to give to me, and how wonderful that felt. The outcome was a feeling of

- being heard
- being understood
- cooperation
- kindness and consideration

With these traits present in my relationships, each of us in the relationship was

inspired to WANT to give more to each other!

This discovery changed my life! I was in control, and I was creating the relationships I wanted. They weren't happening TO me. I was happening to them. Each time I practiced, I got better and better results, and soon, it started to become instinctive. Success was happening at last – not haphazardly, but because I was doing the something different that was creating it. With ME in control, with ME creating the results I wanted, I now knew I COULD be safe AND vulnerable.

There's a quote in Dr. John Demartini's book, *The Heart Of Love*, that inspired me upon first reading it. It sums up what I am saying in one sentence:

"There is an art and a science to asking in a way that inspires an unreserved YES!"

Anyone can do it. Yes, it's an art, but it's also a science. So anyone can learn to do. It only takes practice to make progress.

Although I was getting great direct results with this new insight, I was also benefiting from peripheral results. Giving up my manipulations for a better method was generating more successful thoughts inside of me. As my negative, draining thoughts about life gave way, I automatically smiled more at those around me. Petty annoyances about them began to matter less and less. My nagging, bullying and whining dwindled without effort. I found myself listening more, asking more questions and consequently, understanding more. The result? The world around me was becoming more peaceful.

But had the world around me changed? No! It was me who had changed. Becoming happier myself, I had a more positive effect on other people's lives. The people around me then responded to me differently. The feedback I started to get was one of admiration and appreciation. I was creating a piece of world peace with each person I came in contact with! That too was feeding back into MY happiness. It was becoming an upward spiral, a positive catch-22!

You too can create peace through happiness in your life. As you take responsibility for making yourself happier, you affect the people around you with happiness. And that begins to ripple out in far reaching effects you will never know. When the sphere of life around you increases in peace, it brings additional peace into YOUR life. So what more important mission could you undertake than a peaceful planet by way of your own happiness?

What others do affects your life as much as what you do affects theirs. Happy people don't terrorize your life. Happy people take care of and tend to the planet you live in. Happy people are more productive. Happy people are healthier and spread less sickness. Happy people lay less judgment and condemnation on the people you know. Thus happy people make YOUR world a more comfortable place to live in. Just like your happiness does for them.

And those who are deeply, consciously happy can reach out in compassion to others in pain because they get it – that lashing out in negative behavior comes from a place of hurt and pain. Since merely punishing negative behavior reinforces pain, those that get it know it's important to go beyond just mere behavior control. Getting to the heart of the problem -- the hurt and the pain – is how to fix broken people so they heal and become productive and peaceful members of society once again.

Summing up, can you see how taking charge of making yourself happy, gifts the world the most precious thing you have to give – and in return, gifts back to you?

Then what is the real solution to creating better relationships in your life? Start with your most important, core relationship, the one you love most or want to love more, and try this:

Close your eyes for a moment, and see if you can IMAGINE a relationship with a partner where

- you felt completely loved,
- dramas faded away into compassionate understanding,
- you got your needs met with a unreserved YES!!

Can you picture what kind of excitement you might feel when your workday is done and it's time to come home to or meet up with this loved one?

What could stop such a harmonious connection from going on and on and on? So, from a common sense perspective, could the solution to relationship failure really be this simple?

As you get excited about this, does another part of you step in and wonder, "*Yeah, but can such a relationship even be possible – except for those one-in-ten-thousand that stumble upon their soul's mate?*" Yes, I admit that most of us do try one relationship after another. Common sense knows that most of those end in apathy, judgment or anger. So we never know if our next trial is going to turn out to be the one we have been dreaming and hoping for since we can't predict our future predicaments.

But, what if there is a way to control the outcome? Think about why this lover wanted to be in a relationship with you in the first place. They wanted to feel loved; they wanted to get their needs met; and they wanted to nest in peace. And what about you? Didn't you want the same? That being the case, then if a simple solution could be found to love dying, getting needs met with a smile and ending fighting,

who wouldn't want to stay put in THAT kind of relationship every day, year after year?

What typically happens over the first couple of years though is petty annoyances start to become more prevalent, resentments start to build up, and fighting drains you and your partner from feeling seen and heard. Without simple solutions for keeping this from happening, the result is either a break up or a resignation that this is the way it is, or even worse, that this is love.

But is this actually necessary? And once it happens, is the only solution to find someone else who is a better match? How many times

13

do we need to waste time in this loop before we get wise enough to realize that we need something new?

Think about this: If a simple enough practice could be found that would keep love from dying, wouldn't *petty annoyances disappear*? If a simple enough practice could be found that would get your needs met with a big, hearty YES, wouldn't the buildup of *resentments disappear*? And if a simple enough practice could be found that would give you eyes to see behind the curtain of your fights, wouldn't *compassion and peace reign*? Without petty annoyances and resentments and fighting disintegrating the sizzle in your relationships, and with the joy that comes from feeling fully loved, getting needs met with an unreserved yes, and peaceful communication, how could it not be possible then that *ANYONE* couldn't

CREATE a relationship they loved instead of waiting to stumble into a loving relationship?

The long laundry list of solutions that traditional therapy gives (like treat your partner with respect, don't go to bed mad, listen better, recognize your partner's bid for connection, never lie, be more vulnerable, give more sex, show affection, smile more, and on and on) can be replaced because they only tackle the symptoms, not the causes. If traditional therapy was simple enough to execute, society wouldn't have a 50% or more divorce rate, now would it? But getting to the ROOT CAUSE of WHY we resist doing these things (even after making pacts to do so) is by far more universal and also simple enough to execute. Nourishing the soil these problems grow in will get you faster and more effective results. Guaranteed.

There's an old saying: *When the student is ready, the teacher appears.* When I finally grasped these new ideas for myself, then I knew what I wanted. I was ready. Being ready, I was drawn to the simpler, better answers. Soon it felt like creating a simpler solution to

14

make everyone's life easier was my mission in life, my whole purpose for coming to planet earth. And now, I want this wonderful discovery to be a part of your life. When your life is happier, you create happiness all around you. That benefits me too, just like my happiness does for you.

What I came to know is that your happy relationships are not lost to apathy, anger and separation because relationships are rocket science. They are lost because you simply lack the knowledge of what YOU are doing that is eroding your x's & o's into exes and woes.

With the *right* knowledge, though, your new-relationship sizzle no longer needs to fade into apathy or separation. Or, if you're willing to give it a little time, you can rekindle what you lost. And that is what I am so excited to give you too: this simpler knowledge that will keep your happy glow glowing for years to come.

Then you no longer have to wait for your Prince or Princess Charming (nowadays known as your soul mate), because you can CREATE a blissful relationship. With the *right* knowledge, your vulnerability can safely give up its defenses and allow your heart to have the love it so longs for.

So ask yourself, when is now the right time for you to stop suffering as a victim at the hands of others, and learn to create your own relationship of love? If you feel excited, then applying your learning and practice time efficiently is what this book is all about. As you practice its 3 best practices, you'll be able to watch your relationships change before your very eyes! I did!

You can either have love and connection or you can be right.

Marshal Rosenberg,
Non-Violent Communication

CHAPTER 3
HOW MUCH EFFORT IS REALLY NEEDED?

"*If I find the right one, isn't it supposed to just be easy?*" When discussing relationship solutions, it's common for me to hear someone give me this objection. Women are especially susceptible to this idea. Modern movies and novels still present Mr. Charming whisking them off into happily ever after. Have you used this objection yourself?

My answer comes from one of the known principals of the universe that Isaac Newton, a precursor to Einstein, put forth. Paraphrased, it informs us:

> *All things go from order to disorder unless a force acts upon them.*

This includes relationships.

On one side, are you complaining that a good relationship should just fall into place? And yet, on the other side of your logic, are you acknowledging that anything worth doing, takes learning and skill? Based on this contradiction, I'm willing to bet that what underlies this common complaint is *not* the amount of work, but rather the *lack of results* your efforts have gotten you so far. If you find this contradiction to be true for you too, then let me ask you a question. Would you be open to facing this conflict and ignoring it

if the amount of work necessary to get results could be *simplified* for you, and if your efforts got you maximum results?

CHAPTER 4
MINIMAL EFFORT FOR SPECTACULAR RESULTS

Just how much work is really necessary to get spectacular results? Well, imagine again a relationship where
- you felt fully loved
- dramas and fighting disappeared
- you got your needs met with an unreserved yes!

What could life throw at you to drive you away from such a happy relationship? After all, isn't this the whole reason you got into relationships in the first place? Didn't you have needs you wanted to meet (like being soothed when you hurt, supported when you need a hand, sex, companionship, raising kids, sharing the work load, etc.)? And didn't you want to feel the thrill of being in love? And didn't you want to come home everyday to a peaceful nest with a partner who was happy to see you?

Could it be possible then that your relationship failures can be resolved as simply as focusing on keeping love alive, ending your dramas and getting your needs met? Could it be possible to reduce the myriad of online relationship strategies to just 3 -- if those 3 got you the result of feeling loved, peaceful conflict resolution and your needs met with a smile?

If you are grasping the power of this, wouldn't any amount of work you put into this be worth – well priceless? However, can you see how focusing your efforts on just THREE things, versus the long list of solutions traditional therapy offers, could SIMPLIFY your efforts and streamline your progress?

If you are getting this, it means that you are ready to CREATE your own loving relationship; you CAN BUILD a relationship you love to be in love with now! With the knowledge on how to create

- feeling completely loved,
- compassionate communication versus fighting, and
- getting your needs met with an unreserved yes

you too can get sparkling results. How priceless is that?

CHAPTER 5
TAKING CONTROL

Feeling completely loved, ending the fighting and dramas and getting your needs met with an unreserved yes all have their roots in one word: *communication*. Yes, it is no more complicated than discovering how to speak differently! You see, what you may not be realizing until now is what

you are communicating that is getting you the feedback that you are receiving.

If you are like most people, you will tend to judge other's behavior on their actions and words, rather than on their true intentions. However, for yourself, you will tend to judge your own actions and words on your intentions behind your behavior. When you blend your intentions with your words, it makes it more difficult for you to hear what words you could have chosen to get the feedback you actually wanted. Knowing what you intended to say (vs what is being heard), makes it easier to blame your listener for misunderstanding or not getting you. Considering this then, it would be common for you to think that your partner is the one that needs to change (by listening better). Here's where I'd like to caution you that

trying to get your partner to do the changing by seeing things your way is a slow and tedious process to finding love, ending dramas, and getting your needs met.

The more effective solution is to take control of your own words and learn how to actually communicate what it is you are truly trying to say (versus what is being heard). Learning from your feedback what you could do more, better, different or less to communicate your thoughts brings misunderstandings and resistances back under *your* control. The result is communication that is clearer for your listener and definitely more effective.

If I am honest with myself and with you, I'd have to admit that I created my own heartbreak – unwittingly (in the break up I shared with you in chapter one). I seriously did not want my partner to leave me. I did everything I could to mend the wedge between us. But it was of no use; I had lacked the knowledge I needed to create the relationship I actually wanted. I had created a relationship of pain, and now I had to endure the pain. I felt like a victim, not understanding how I could have prevented such a loss. All I could do was wish and hope and cry.

I never want to feel like such a victim again. So I made it my mission to **put the control into my own hands**. By looking for the way to take personal responsibility for my communications, I uncovered the knowledge to create my outcome. I then stopped ignorantly stumbling through my relationships, just blaming my listeners for being short sighted or not listening well.

And now I extend the same invitation to you. Do you want to give up being a victim to your own lack of knowledge? Do you want to create a relationship that you and your partner will want to come home to over and over again for many years to come? Only in having control can you diminish your risk of failure completely. Fear-based tactics like avoidance and sabotage will no longer be necessary. Feelings of impending doom that it's all going to fall apart can ebb away. Only in this safe feeling will your vulnerability be willing let your heart have the connection it so longs for.

If you are excited about the possibility, then it's time to turn your attention to learning the 3 best practices that will prevent your X's & O's from becoming exes and woes.

CHAPTER 6
THE OVERVIEW

As the last 5 chapters you read have shown, relationship failure can be narrowed down to just 3 root causes:

- love dying,
- bargaining for needs and
- unresolved fighting

With this new acceptance, then only 3 practices, 3 BEST practices, (that solve the problem of love dying, needs and dramas) are needed to turn your prior failure into future SUCCESS! That certainly simplifies things and makes success easier to secure. This simplified solution is what will be covered in the remainder of your reading.

This book will be giving you enough detail to ensure you know not only *what* to do, but *how* to do it. But before we get into the *details* on how you can install the 3 practices for love, needs and dramas into your life, wouldn't it be nice to have a quick overview? That way, you can have a general awareness of each problem and its solution before you begin. Haven't you always found it easier to absorb the details if you see the big picture first?

And are you remembering, this chapter is just the <u>aerial view</u>, OK?

PROBLEM #1
YOU SAY YOU LOVE ME, SO WHY DON'T I FEEL LOVED?

Isn't the most obvious issue that plagues any relationship, the loss of the honeymoon stage? You were once madly in love – and now your sizzle has turned into apathy. Can't a dozen therapeutic perspectives be found online to make this loss digestible? But what if we think outside the box therapy has given us? What if this loss is simply not necessary?

Let's start by asking why eliminating this loss is so important. Petty annoyances are why. Someone whose love tank is full doesn't care if you put down the toilet seat, or if you are often late, or if you have an odd, quirky behavior or expression, true? Those things are just *"cute"* when you are newly in love, right? After the honeymoon stage fades, however, these same *"cute"* traits become annoying, a cause for eye rolling, mocking, guilting or even anger. Perhaps they even refer to you as stifling, like some kind of old ball and chain.

As you listen back to old conversations in your memories, can you recall the times you thought you were being loving, only to hear your partner respond with some mocking or guilting response that showed you that they didn't think so? Can you recall how you felt a need to defend yourself, perhaps with a comment like, *"Well I show love by (fill in the blank)."*

This is because there is a basic tendency by people to think

everyone feels loved in the same way.

What this means is that your partner tends to love you the way *they* like being loved. The same is true about you. You tend to love your partner the way *you* like being loved. When this assumption is inserted into your relationship, it is easy to become baffled when your partner complains. What follows is typically a thought that sounds something like, *"Well, since I know I'm really loving in this relationship, it can't be ME! And if not me, well it has to be the only other person in this relationship!"*

Sound familiar? Here is the resolution I came to:

People have a need to FEEL loved, not just BE loved.

Gary Chapman's book, *The 5 Love Languages*, teaches that there are 5 ways that love is given, so there are also 5 ways that love is received. More importantly, people have one or two of these 5 ways that are *PRIMARY* to them. His book goes on to say that

people only *FEEL* fully loved when they are loved in *THEIR PRIMARY* way.

Without being loved in *their* primary way, they will be left feeling empty. Everyone knows that an empty love tank is the source of nagging, mocking, guilting, eye rolling, and angry annoyance. Would anyone need to be convinced that when this type of criticism enters the relationship that love fades?

Therefore, the simple solution is to

spend your love time learning your partner's way of receiving love, and practice daily how to speak it.

And vice versa. Then both of you can *build* love into your relationship. With the controls in *your* own hands, you can *create* the loving bond you have dreamed of (rather than waiting for your dreams to come true). More smiles are your immediate payoff, and keeping that new relationship sizzle long after the honeymoon phase is your long-term payoff. Who wouldn't be motivated to gain all that?

PROBLEM #2
YOU WANT ME TO SACRIFICE MY SELFISH DESIRES?
IN ORDER TO MEET YOUR (SELFISH) DESIRES?

The struggle it takes to try and get your needs met is the next biggest disappointment in relationships. You enter your relationship with such high hopes that this lover is *"going to fulfill me, save me, provide for my happiness."* Your eyes sparkle with the thought of how this new person is *"going to do this thing and going to do that thing that makes me feel so complete."* You just know that *"happily ever after"* is on the horizon. And then, time goes by, and you can't help but recognize that your partner really isn't so interested in doing all those things to fulfill your life, are they? And neither are you for them, really, are you?

And what is the old handed-down practice for responding to this? Accusations and guilt, right? This is so prevalent in our society, it would be rare for you to have escaped this manipulation. If you are like most people, from the beginning of your life, if you didn't do what your parents or your church or your culture -- and then your relationships -- wanted from you, you were accused of not caring enough, of being *selfish,* weren't you?

But how can sacrificing "your *selfish* desires", so those making the request of you can have their (selfish) desires met, be done from your heart? And if not done from your heart, how can such sacrifices be rewarding or satisfying?

I know I am treading on sacred ground here, so don't get me wrong. There is no doubt that love also sacrifices. If someone leaps in front of a bullet to save your life, that's love doing that – for sure!

Yet too often the sacrifice given in relationships is really motivated by acquiescence, not love, especially if the work to keep love alive has yet to be done. What is acquiescence? Giving in, in order to avoid further argument. You don't want the drama, so you *"pick your battles*", or you try to play fair by *"compromising"* – *"I'll give in here if you give in there."* One of my clients even told me that he and his partner kept score! If you are honest with yourself, your brain may convince you that this is love, but surely your heart knows better!

Acquiescence is the #1 reason behind most of the sacrifices your partner does for you. It is also the #1 reason why you do the same. You want peace. You want to choose your battles. So you acquiesce. So does your partner. Many of you have let me know this idea triggers you. If you need to block this simple truth, and cling to idealistic ideas, it just means that you are not ready for simplifying your relationship problems yet. There are many relationship strategies that all lead to the same end; some just take longer. So I invite you just hear me out before you turn away to a longer path.

Why does this sacrifice-to-show-me-you-love-me model break down? Why does the end result not lead to that loving connection society says it should? Here is the resolution I came to:

Sacrifice, not done in love, breeds resentment.

This old, win-lose idea of *sacrifice-your-needs-for-my-needs,* that was handed down by the older generation, leaves the giving partner feeling obligated. How can giving out of obligation ever feel good to the giver or the recipient?

And everyone knows what the result of feeling obligated is, right? Resentments. Would anyone need to be convinced that a build up of resentments leads to relationship failure?

Holding unresolved resentments inside can't lead anywhere but to mistrust! And how can mistrust cause anything but a pulling away from your partner and your partner from you? Stored resentments are the #2 cause, in my opinion, of the gradual decline in passion and romance, and that leads to relationship failure. Therefore, it is essential to keeping a relationship happy and with a long life, that a new, more innovative solution be discovered! A solution that will

- keep peace *and*
- get your needs met *and*
- not get you accused of being selfish

will get your heart the result it actually wants, an unreserved YES from your partner!

That leads us to the question: how can you ask your partner for your needs to be met that leaves them *wanting* to say yes to you? First, let me share a valuable truth that will support my solution:

People will CHOOSE to act
when it is in accordance with their own HIGHEST values.

This is a common statement of fact I have heard in several different certified trainings I have taken. If you question its validity, try considering whether it is the *highest* value you are not quite catching on to.

How can you apply this then to this second problem? When you ask someone to do something that is in alignment with THEIR values, they respond more willingly. People will always find a way to do something that they really value. Knowing this can create a *WIN-WIN* solution if

you ask for your needs to be met through your partner's value
system!

Remember the quote from Dr. John Demartini's book, *The Heart of Love?*

"There is an art and a science to asking in such a way, that it inspires an unreserved YES".

PROBLEM #3
FIGHTING WITH YOU MAKES ME FEEL SO UNSEEN!

When issues around love and needs did not take down the failed relationships I studied, it was because they succumbed to this one last thing. I call this one last thing *traumas and dramas*. This is where you look at your partner in disbelief that he or she could have said what they just did. Then the both of you end up in this escalating battle, each trying to pull the other to your own mindset. The result is confusion that your partner can be so unreasonable, leaving you frustrated with angry feelings coursing through your veins.

Sound familiar? So, what do you need to know better, so you can do better? In these types of arguments, what you are encountering is

a defense.

Although these defenses are being triggered by a current event, they are not connected to it. Your partner is having his or her buttons pushed. This means that they are merely reacting to a trigger that is igniting a decades-old defense created for some early childhood trauma. These defenses were created so far back in their childhood, that they don't even know why they react the way they do anymore. The defense reacts by either disconnecting, collapsing, withdrawing, over exerting, or getting rigid. Your attempts at communicating then turn into an argument. And you tuck away the experience into your heart as another example of not being seen, heard nor understood – and wanting to blame your partner for this.

It's not one-sided either. This whole process is also going on with your partner about you.

Isn't trying to get your partner to adapt their behavior to prevent your buttons from being pushed a difficult task? How would you like to manage this reaction instead?

What You Need To Know First

First, let's look at how this all got started. There are 5 basic developmental periods from pre-birth through puberty that all children go through. Each stage is a breeding ground for a common trauma. By common, I mean that it's normal for most kids to go through the experience. When a child is exposed to this common trauma, the child defends itself by creating a defensive wall. This is also common.

Being common, this means that your partner was also exposed to all 5 developmental stages. Creating a defensive wall was a normal way for your partner to protect his or herself. It was their inner child's way to adapt to each of their traumas and create safety during a time when their mind was too young and inexperienced to do differently.

Unfortunately, these defenses were carried into their adult lives where, behind the scenes, they wreak havoc with your relationship. They continue to be attached to your partner's inner child, not their adult mind, so no longer serve them like they did when they were little. That is why it feels so natural to say to your partner in an argument, *"Grow up!"*

But, by learning about the origins of your partner's defenses, and how their present-day triggers are connected to these defenses, you can make a more CONSCIOUS reaction. Conscious reactions avoid the unconscious results of this carry over. Then statements like *"This is stupid! Grow up!"* no longer seem necessary. Neither does agonizing over, *"Why is my partner acting this way?"* Awareness can allow curiosity to replace your frustration. By understanding that a defense is being triggered behind your partner's responses, you take charge and MANAGE the result instead of being a victim to its confusion and anger.

The simple solution then is to

observe which defense is being triggered when your partner seems unreasonable, and then use the best response to soothe that defense.

The result is communication that is fulfilling and gets to your desired result – instead of fighting. The payoff is less drama, fewer hurt feelings, and being seen and understood. How priceless is that!

We're going to get into the details of what all this means and how to make it work for you in the subsequent chapters. For now, this chapter is meant to just give you a quick overview. So, if you are ready, then let's get to it!

PRACTICE #1

FEELING THE LOVE

CHAPTER 7
THE HEART NEEDS TO FEEL LOVED, NOT JUST BE LOVED

Love! It brings you to the heights of joy and into the depths of despair. Everyone, I mean everyone, seems to love love. When it happens to you, your heart swells up, you smile more, and you care about the little annoyances less. True? Heck, when you are in love, forgiving everyone around you for anything is easy, isn't it?

So why is it so difficult to keep it glowing? Why can't you be excited about the one you fall in love with for a lifetime? Why can't your partner be excited about you for a lifetime?

The solution is hidden in this little known secret that no one ever told you:

The human heart needs to *feel* loved, not just *be* loved.

It's just a slight tweak in perception, isn't it? But the change to the end result is immense. The thing you may be doing, unwittingly, is giving acts of love to your partner – but without taking into consideration *your partner's* love values. We all do it. We assume, and then we give love the way we like to receive love.

"Well, of course I do," you might be saying right now. *"What's wrong with that? I'm loving, aren't I? Shouldn't my partner see that?"* Yes, your partner most likely does see that. And yet, for some reason, feeling loved is still not the end result of your efforts. You see, the heart needs to *FEEL* loved, not just *BE* loved.

So what can you know better in order to do better? You love another the way you like to be loved. Sounds reasonable, right? After

all, isn't love just love?
No!

CHAPTER 8
ONE'S PRIMARY LOVE LANGUAGE

Loving another person the way you like to be loved simply doesn't work – maybe not all the time, but a LOT of the time. Why is that?

There are 5 different ways to show another person that you love them. Therefore, there are 5 different ways another person takes in love. Each person values *one* of those 5 ways the *most* – and is a tad more indifferent to the other 4.

If you do your favored way of feeling loved toward your partner, they will feel somewhat loved, but their internal critic will still complain. Given time, comments about not feeling loved will begin to show up in their conversations -- unless, of course, you happen to stumble upon a partner that feels loved the same way you do. Stumbling upon such a person may make this aspect of a relationship easier for you, but it could also leave you flipping through a lot of trial relationships. If you don't want to wait to stumble across someone with the same love language, it would be best to consider this better option.

Here is the important key:

Unless one is loved in *their* primary way, their love tank will not feel full.

And not *feeling* loved is the fertile soil that grows the weeds of petty annoyances, guilting, nit picking, eye-rolling and mocking. So if you want to avoid this and ensure your partner *feels* all the love you have for them long after your honeymoon stage, then you need to learn to speak *their* primary love language, and you need to do it *daily*.

If you mastered just this *one* practice, you would have achieved the #1 cornerstone of all great relationships. You would have the most important building block that would get you through a multitude of other errors, and bring peace and contentment to your relationship.

If you could learn to identify your partner's *primary* love value, and learn to speak that language of love daily, how much change do you think you could bring to your partner's feeling of being loved? And what about you? If your partner could learn to speak daily within your primary love value, how full would your love tank start to feel?

A favored example of mine is that of a wife complaining about not feeling loved by her husband. The husband is astonished, saying, *"But, honey, I tell you all the time how beautiful you are and how much I appreciate and love you! What do you mean?"* To which, she responds, *"Yes, but you never get off your lazy ass and help me."* He is speaking words-of-affirmation, his favored love language, and even though she likes that, her love tank is not full. What she needs to feel full is acts-of-service, a different love language than what her husband is lovingly giving her.

Do you think her husband gives her words of affirmation instead of acts of service because he is uncaring? Heck no! He does it because he is simply blind to the fact that she has a different way of feeling fully loved, and *assumes* she receives loving feelings the same way he does.

That being true, do you think that once he becomes aware that this is common between couples, and he replaces his assumption with this important knowledge, that he would not gladly choose a better option? He obviously loves his wife. So chances are, the answer is yes! He just doesn't know this simple fact of how the human heart works, not just for his wife, but also for everyone, and that this simple piece of knowledge mattered so much it could keep true love from fading. He was believing in his heart that he *was* loving his wife. Therefore, if his wife wasn't feeling it, the fault must lie in her. That is – until he becomes knowledgeable about how primary love languages affect the heart. Isn't this important for you to discover too?

Now flip it around and try considering the impact on his life if he chooses to continue to show his love only with words of affirmation *OR* if he chooses to add acts of service. If his wife feels fully loved, how is she going to speak to him? How is she going to look at him? How willingly is she going to forgive behaviors that annoyed her before? Hmmm... This is well worth considering, true?

So the first thing I invite you to observe is that your partner's primary love language may well be different than yours! If you happen to stumble into a relationship with a person who has the same primary love language as yourself, well that makes things simpler. But if not, does that mean that a relationship with this awesome person is impossible? Of course not! You just need to spend the attention needed to discover your partner's primary love language, and *learn to speak it*!

How simple is that excellent use of your efforts! And what conversation can be more fun in the beginning of any relationship than exploring each other's love languages?

CHAPTER 9
5 COMMUNICATIONS FOR
FILLING A LOVE TANK

To gain a clearer insight into love languages, I invite you to read Gary Chapman's book. I believe he has one geared towards married couples and one geared towards singles. But in the meantime, here is the list and a short blurb to get you started:

1. **WORDS OF AFFIRMATION – Tell Your Partner**
    Some people glow when you tell them how much you love, care for, congratulate or appreciate them. This form of love acts as music to their ears.

2. **GIFTS – Bring Your Partner**
    Some people glow when you give them an actual, tangible gift. This form of love delights their eyes and sends a message to their heart each and every time they see it.

3. **QUALITY TIME – Date Your Partner**
    Some people glow when you spend time, with focused attention, on them. For example, a dinner date, a game night, a road trip, a picnic or sharing a book together are some common ways of doing this. This form of love gives them a deep feeling of being seen, heard and valued.

4. **ACTS OF SERVICE – Help Your Partner**
    Some people glow when you identify something they need done and either do it for them, or help them do it. For example,

repairing something, doing a task or helping with a project are common. This form of love gives them a sense of being supported.

5. **TOUCH – Pet Your Partner**
   Some people glow when you reach out and touch them – appropriately of course. The way you touch another person carries a lot of communication with it. Have you ever had someone wake you up with a gentle stroke or, conversely, with a poke of their finger? It sends a different message, doesn't it? The way someone chooses to touch you communicates how they are feeling inside about you. Loving touch gives a sense of connection.

CHAPTER 10
LEARNING TO HEAR LOVE

Now, your task is to go through the 5 languages and rank their value from 1 to 5. One important side remark: try not to be too quick to decide that you know what the love language is. If you spend the time questioning each one, you may be surprised to discover your first thoughts change. I certainly found that to be true.

Here are some helpful tips that will give you the clues you need:

- Listen for the stories that your partner tells about something someone did that warmed their heart.
- Listen for complaints about others, connected to what is not being received.
- Listen for the things they notice in a movie or in a book they are reading.
- Listen to the comments they make about the relationships of their friend's or colleague's.

What theme comes up again and again? Is it touch? Is it gifts? Is it acts of service? Quality time? Compliments or other affirmations?

And don't you need to do the same for yourself – stand aside and listen to your own stories, complaints and comments – and see what language they are pointing to? After all, you are half of the relationship, aren't you? Are you recognizing that both partners need to feel loved, not just be loved?

Remember – all 5 love languages speak love to everyone. What you are looking for is the PRIMARY one. So as you go through this exercise, notice which one repeats itself the most.

Practice #1: Feeling The Love

For more help obtaining this critically important piece of information, you could take the test at

https://www.5lovelanguages.com/quizzes/

CHAPTER 11
LEARNING TO SPEAK LOVE

It is in learning to speak your loved one's primary love language that you light up his or her life, and develop that secure bond of friendship and love. Every ounce of practice you and your partner put into this cornerstone will bring you closer and closer to building a relationship you will love to stay in love with.

Once you know what the language is that you want to learn, here is an excellent tip for you: think about, collect and write down 20 different ways that you could speak that language to your partner. And have your partner do the same in return for you. Make each item on the list simple to do, not elaborate. The simpler to do, the better. Why? Because simplicity makes it more likely that you will practice speaking the language. As one of my mentors, Maurice DiMino says, *"practice makes progress"*. And simplicity promotes practice.

Here are some examples to show you how simple this can be:

WORDS OF AFFIRMATION
- On a sticky note, write something like *"you fill my heart with gladness"* or *"thank you for loving me"* or *"I love you"*. Then put it on the inside of the mirror your partner opens in the morning. Or, attach it to a credit card in their wallet such that they will find it when they go to pay for something. Or put it under their pillow to find when they go to bed, especially if you are going to be gone. Even if they read this book, and know these ideas, they will still enjoy it.
- Being seen for the good that we are can rocket anyone to the moon. Try appreciating something you love about your partner. For example:

42

"I love the way you laugh at my jokes."
"Thank you for picking up the (ice cream or kale) I so enjoy."
"Thank you for being so sweet to my mother."
"You have a good heart. I appreciate the kindness you showed to ..."
"You take really good care of (this family, our garden, the car). Thank you."
"You are like my knight in shiny armor."

- Try changing general words in your sentence to more specific words. For example:
  "Dinner was great honey." → *"That spice in the rice was delicious. What was it?"*
  "You are so pretty/handsome to me." → *"Your blue eyes move me"* or *"Your smile lights up a room"* or *"I love the way you wear your hair"* or *"I find the way your muscles ripple really hot"* or *"The hair on your arms feels so masculine to me"*.
- If you are out of town, take a picture of something interesting and text it to your partner, along with a wish that they could have been there to share it.
- After settling into your sleeping position, say something sweet like, *"thanks for being you"*, smile in your heart, then go to sleep.
- Congratulate your partner on an achievement or a job well done: *"Wow, you did that!"*
- Remember when giving a gift for a special occasion, it's the words you write in the card that will matter the most.

GIFTS

- Pay attention and write down for a period of time all the things that your partner directly or indirectly says they would like or would want. I do this on their address card in my phone in the Notes section, or on my phone's Notepad app. I always have my phone with me, so I always have the list. Purchase something small and not too costly on the list. Then, on a no-occasion day, pop in excited and say that you found this (thing), and just thought they would like to have it. It doesn't even have to be wrapped.

- If you are out of town, bring something home for them, and say *"I was thinking of you"*.
- Of course, you never want to miss a holiday or special event like a birthday. So be sure to calendar these events with a pop-up reminder a week or two ahead.
- If wrapped, gifts should be pleasing to the eye, a teaser of what is to come. This adds excitement. Get a friend or salesperson to help if needed.
- Receiving a gift that is in alignment with their values, makes the gift all the more special. You can uncover their values with these ideas:
  - o Listen to what subject your partner loves to draw a conversation into. Is it work, sports, family, spiritual pursuits, a hobby, culture, nature, travel?
  - o Listen to what they tell their friends they got from someone.
  - o Look around their space, and see what objects they keep around them.
  - o Look at their style: are they streamlined, frilly, earthy, luxurious, homey?
  - o Look at the colors they wear or that they surround themselves with.

If the objects you choose are within your partner's values, their style, and their colors, you will increase the degree the gift fills their love tank.

Practice #1: Feeling The Love

QUALITY TIME

- Invite your partner on a date. Tell them how to dress, and the time you will pick them up. You could splash in a pool together. Or you could go sight seeing, stopping along the way at an interesting market to buy sandwiches, then stop at a park or an interesting vista to eat and chat.
- Thumb through a stack of magazines together noting words or pictures of things that interest each other. You could cut these out and paste them into an arrangement on heavy stock paper, then discuss the message it sends.
- Go for a stroll together or take some wine and cheese and a blanket and watch the sunset together.
- Read a book together, discussing interesting points as you go along.
- Have an interactive game night. You could play video games, go bowling, play tennis or pool, gin rummy or monopoly.
- Go on a road trip or train trip together.
- If you are really pressed for time, you could even wash dishes together!
- For a special event, forego the tangible gift and give them an experience to remember instead. You could take them somewhere interactive like an arcade, or amusement park, or to a wine or cooking class, to a paint night, a festival, or to a dance, just to name a few.

ACTS OF SERVICE

- Ask your partner how you can support them in a project they are working on – like doing a small piece of something bigger that will save them a little time.
- Quiz or rehearse with your partner something they are trying to learn or memorize – or let them teach it to you.

- Surprise them by doing a chore for them like taking the trash out or washing the dishes or making the bed or watering the plants or getting their car cleaned.
- Go through your partner's To Do list with them. Then pick anything, no matter how small, and tell them you will take care of that task for them.
- For a special event, give them a coupon that grants them a specific or open-ended request. If you have limitations on when, where or how, be sure to add, *"Can be used (limits)."*

TOUCH

- As you walk by your partner while they're doing a task, wrap your arms around them from the back and just squeeze and hold 5-10 seconds. Then just smile, looking them in the eye, giving a light squeeze to their arm as you walk off without a word.
- As you lie down to go to bed, reach over and hold your partner's hand, and lightly squeeze it for 5-10 seconds. Words are not necessary.
- Ask to wash your partner's back when in the shower, or dry them off afterwards.
- Manicure your partner's nails at home, or wash their hair or rub lotion into their hands, scratch their back or head or give them a massage.
- While sitting with them, watching the TV or listening to music, lay your head on their shoulder, or place your hand in theirs, or have them put their head in your lap and lightly stroke them.
- If you are sitting across from them at a table, place your socked foot lightly atop theirs.
- As a gift for a special occasion, give a spa treatment, a pedicure or a massage.

Practice #1: Feeling The Love

There are hundreds more ideas within each language. My goal is to show you how simple it is to learn to speak a language that may not be your own primary language. It doesn't have to be complicated nor expensive to make it say "*I love and care about you*". It just has to be thoughtful and sincere. And it is always thoughtful if it is spoken in your partner's primary love language.

The key lies in paying attention! This is a really fun way to make your partner feel seen in a meaningful and useful way – in a way that works for your relationship. And vice versa. It is in learning to speak your partner's primary language that you light up his or her life. Every ounce of practice you put into this will reward you with a closer bond. So once you know the language you want to learn, keep a list of ideas. Make the list simple; the simpler the better, and the more likely you are to practice. And as you've already heard, practice makes progress!

CHAPTER 12
LETTING GO OF THE MASK

The best thing about you and your partner feeling really loved is that you both become more forgiving. Then, without daily criticisms coming at you, you tend to let go of your masks and be more authentic with each other. There is something very soothing, releasing and relaxing about being able to "*let your hair down*" and be seen for who you really are. Isn't that a big win for both of you?

To sum up, without small annoyances eroding at or driving wedges between you and your partner, wouldn't you be more apt to live and let live? You may have struggled with letting annoyances lie, so you may have used the more commonly-taught tool of "*picking your battles.*" But what if you simply weren't annoyed – like when you first met? Wouldn't that be awesome!

It is a common fact that when you and your partner feel fully loved, you are so much more open to just let the little things go – and from the heart. And that lays the groundwork for acceptance. Don't you feel you can be more authentic when you feel fully accepted? Being authentic leads to being seen, loved and appreciated for who you are. And there is nothing more satisfying than that, is there? Who would ever want to leave a relationship like that? So, what a wonderful practice to practice practice practice!

This is the easiest of the practices needed to build relationships that work. And if this essential practice is studied together, what can be more fun and more bonding in a relationship than focusing on love?

So I recommend that it be the first and most important cornerstone that you put into place – together.
Remember:

The heart needs to *feel* loved, not just *be* loved.

CHAPTER 13
LOVE COMES FIRST

M y goal is to help you build a relationship that works because joy will fill your *own* life! And that will spill over onto the individuals around you, enriching everyone you come in contact with, as well as your own primary relationship.

Successful implementation is key! If you try to focus on too many new practices at the same time, you stand the risk of implementing poorly and becoming discouraged and giving up. The simplest way to prevent that dilemma is to *focus only on one practice at a time and master it until it becomes habit.* Then move to the next, and so forth.

Would you be willing to forego moving onto needs and dramas and just practice the love language until you are happy with the progress you have made? If your relationship is new, this can be easy and quick. If your relationship is already shifted into apathy, it may take a little more time to build the trust necessary to get the momentum started. But guaranteed that if you practice until you get it to work for you, the effort you put into it will reward your heart and bring joy back into your life.

And then you need to move to practice #2…

PRACTICE #2

GETTING YOUR NEEDS MET

CHAPTER 14
UNSETTING THE STAGE FOR FAILURE

After decades of observation, I noted a fact that *two* people are involved in any communication that creates an unhappy relationship – unwittingly. What this means is that together you are executing, unwittingly, domesticated ideas, hand-me-downs from older generations, ideas that the media propagates because it makes good stories. But as Oprah Winfrey is known to say, *"When we know better, we do better."* When you know better, that's when you can choose your words consciously and give up unconscious words and actions you unwittingly do that drive wedges into your relationships.

What I have seen and heard time and again is that what people expect from families and friends is support through thick and thin. But what they actually expect from lovers, more than anything else, is

to get their needs met.

That means that you go into relationships with the expectation that this lover is going to be your savior, look deep into your eyes and smile, and you will know how much they love you by how much they are willing to sacrifice their own needs for you.

It is common knowledge that people write on their new relationships what their own hopes and needs are, and become disillusioned over time when they begin to notice that their expectations are disappointed.

Give this a little thought, and see if this doesn't apply to you as well.

You see, although the idea of being someone's savior, their all-encompassing everything, sounds so enticing, isn't the weight of it, actually a heavy burden for anyone to carry? Sooner or later, won't you fail to meet your new lover's expectations and they yours? And then what happens? Disappointment? Bickering? That's a sure way to begin to erode any relationship, isn't it?

What typically happens from there? Manipulations in the form of guilting, whining, anger, bargaining or withdrawal are quite common. Does anyone need to be convinced that these types of manipulations will erode the feeling of love in any relationship?

CHAPTER 15
WHAT? YOU'RE CALLING <u>ME</u> SELFISH?

When you ask for your needs to be met by trying to manipulate your partner into giving up their needs, you may whine, get angry, pressure, guilt, or call them names like *"selfish"* – all with the goal of getting your partner to choose your (selfish) needs over their own. Doing this informs your partner that this is how you know they respect and love you – by what they are willing to sacrifice. But when they give in, is it really out of a show of love?

This reminds me of when I was young, and boys would tell us girls, *"If you loved me, you would …"* It wasn't until us girls got smart enough to respond, *"If you loved me, you wouldn't ask"* that this obvious manipulation was stopped in its tracks.

If you have studied the 5 love languages by now, you would know that such manipulations have nothing to do with love. But they still have everything to do with sacrifice. When you receive sacrifices because your partner is trying to avoid further arguments, when you receive sacrifices because our partner is picking their battles, are you actually receiving love? Are you actually receiving respect? Let's open to a little honesty here, can we, and flip it around? How often do you actually sacrifice your needs for someone else out of heart-felt love for them, and how often do you do it because you don't want to *"get into it"* with them?

More often than most of us would like to agree, this so-called *sacrifice-for-love* would be more accurately labeled *acquiescence.* What is acquiescence? It's giving in – in order to avoid further argument. The sacrifice is done only to avoid confrontation, with a hope that the other person buys into it as an act of love.

Here is the problem with this common tactic:

Sacrifice, not done out of love, breeds resentment.

And resentments will drive wedges into your happy love life. Enough wedges, and you will end up feeling alienated and wondering where your love went.

But if you don't know anything else, you are kind of stuck with this age-old method of trying to get your needs met, right? Or are you? What if you knew a better way that

- kept peace *and*
- got your needs met *and*
- didn't get you accused of being selfish?

What if you could learn a way <u>out of</u> compromising your own needs and <u>still</u> be able to fulfill your partner's needs as well? Would you be open to trying something new?

Yes, there is a better way, a win-win way, versus the win-sacrifice way you have been handed down from the old folks. There is a way that actually builds a relationship, instead of manipulates it so gracefully by surrounding the manipulations in acceptable words like *respect* and *love*.

CHAPTER 16
WHAT? WE CAN BOTH WIN?

It should be obvious to anyone over the age of 18 that the partners you have had did not read minds, so you do in fact need to ask for your needs to be met, no matter what technique you use to do that. But is it really necessary to manipulate in order to get your partner to say yes? Isn't the very fact that you feel compelled to manipulate a sign that you are running into resistance? If you are running into resistance, then true desire from the heart is not there, is it? If your partner is acquiescing to your needs, how satisfying is that – really? Given the choice of receiving acquiescence to your manipulations or an unreserved YES, which would you prefer? So if I could share with you a practice that could get your needs met with an unreserved YES, could you be interested in replacing manipulation with it?

Let's look at why manipulation happens. Is it because you love it? I once asked a guy why he lied about his intentions with sex partners. And he answered, *"Because she wouldn't sleep with me if I didn't."* Interesting, I thought. He doesn't lie because he's a natural born liar. He lies because he wants to get his needs met, and he doesn't know another way.

Isn't that true of all your manipulations too? Do you manipulate because it is your nature to be a manipulator? Or do you manipulate because you want your needs met, and you simply don't know how to obtain your desire otherwise?

In the world of NLP[1], it is a truth that when the mind is given increased choices, it will choose the better way. Maybe this is true because the better way is also the path of least resistance? If you could

---

[1] NLP stands for Neuro Linguistic Programming. NLP involves research done over the last 50 years on how the human mind works. A common way to think about it is the *user's guide to the brain.*

discover a more innovative, *win-win* strategy, a way out of this *"sacrifice your selfish needs for my selfish needs"* strategy, could you be willing to try out that new idea instead?

Let's look at this other choice. What possibilities might exist if you were to ask for your needs to be met, but you did it through your partner's value system? Can you stop and ponder that for a moment? In the arena of my studies, it is common knowledge that

**everyone will find the time to do what is in accordance with
THEIR highest values.**

Why? Because it is something they value, of course. If you doubt this, perhaps you are not recognizing the true value that underlies your partner's actions.

Can we take this even further? If you were to ask for your needs to be met by linking that need to your partner's value system, would the recipient of your request not be more willing to give you an unreserved YES because they *want* to, rather than because they are *sacrificing* for you? And does that mutual desire to say yes, not create a win-win for both of you? And without sacrifice, can there be any resultant resentment? And without resentments eroding away at your happiness, isn't it more possible for that loving feeling to last and last?

As Dr. John Demartini said in his book, Heart of Love, *"There's an art and a science to asking in a way that inspires an unreserved YES!"*

One of my favorite examples in John's book is about himself and his wife. He needs to teach for several weeks in another country – Italy I think it was. He could tell his wife he has to leave, that it is his job, and important. But he decides to look at his wife's value system instead. She works for Vogue, and some things she values is sleeping in, shopping and spas. So instead, he tells her he has to go to Italy to teach, but on a particular date, he is going to be in a particular city that has great shopping and spas. He says he would love her to join him there, and asks if she would be willing to do so on that date. He explains she could sleep in while he teaches, then go shopping and spend time in beautiful spas. And then in the evening, they could go out on the town together. Now, instead of being resentful and annoyed about being left for three weeks, she is eagerly looking forward to his trip.

Can you see how getting his needs met by thinking about his wife's values changed the entire dynamic of that conversation? Can you think on how easily that conversation could have gone down the path of anger, shame and blame? But instead, it ended in joy and happiness – and for no other reason than he thought about his wife's values and linked them onto his own need to travel. In this way, he didn't feel a need to hide what he was doing, nor to demand or guilt her into understanding (resentfully). And no one had to sacrifice any needs for the other person's needs. It was a win-win for both of them!

Here is another example a female friend shared with me one day. Karen's home seriously needed an update. However, the family finances, although not bad, were too tight for such extras. Her husband, Cane, had a fancy car that could be replaced with a nice, but economical one, with enough money left over to redo the kitchen and den areas of their home. Yet Cane obstinately refused to let it go, saying he needed it to look successful in the world, and that Karen should understand that. This bothered Karen, as she and Cane both loved hanging out with friends, and yet felt too embarrassed to allow them over. She could have easily said, *"Well, if he cared about my feelings and my life, he would give it up. Home and friends should be more important to him than his dumb car."* She could even go so far as to make up stories about how selfish he was and unloving he must be not to consider her needs too. She could even dump him for not loving her enough if he didn't want to sacrifice such a selfish need. But instead of dumping him or manipulating him into sacrificing something he valued, she appealed to a higher value of his. *"Well, you know,"* she said, *"if we remodeled our guest areas, you could get a pool table and create a man-cave in the den that would wow your buddies, and even your boss. And we could all enjoy pool and movies and games together, wives against husbands. And you know how much our female friends and I love to cook gourmet dinners together. Can you imagine how impressed your boss might be to come over for a dinner party with your friends?"* The next week, the money was in the bank.

Another story I was told was about Mary, a sick wife languishing in the hospital. She wouldn't eat and was not getting any better. Mary's husband was quite upset with her, and he scolded her daily for her selfishness. One day the aunt of the woman in the next bed stopped by, and while chatting with Mary's husband, learned of the situation.

The aunt went home and set about making a special desert for Mary. It was full of vitamins from special fruits the aunt grew in her garden. But there was more to it than that. She also added special flower petals and blessed it. She then put it in a beautifully shaped colored glass bowl, decorated it lovingly with tiny leaves and flowers, and took it to the hospital.

Mary's eyes delighted at what she saw. She had never seen such colorful, pretty food before. She couldn't resist putting her finger into the soft, sweet, cool stuff, and bringing it to her nose to smell it. And then she tasted it. A shudder of delight ran through her. She smiled, and eagerly, hungrily set to eating the entire bowl.

Can you see how there is an art and a science to asking in a way that inspires an unreserved YES!

The key to this practice is in *paying attention* to your partner. It only takes focused attention to look for and identify your partner's values, as I will share with you in the next chapter. What is worth repeating here is that every ounce of practice you and your partner put into this practice will reward you both ten-fold. It worked for John; it worked for Karen and Mary; it works for my students, my clients, and me. I know it can work for you.

Are you remembering that the goal of you reading this book is to simplify the cause of your relationship failures so you can easily build a relationship that works for YOU? And then, I know that the joy you build into each relationship will spread to everyone around you and help make the whole world a brighter place – for me to live in too. This is how I use your values to get my needs met too. It's a win-win for both of us – and everyone else!

CHAPTER 17
DETERMINING VALUES

Nothing influences your partner's decisions and actions more than their internal values. One of the highest relationship values is peace. So your partner may acquiesce to your needs, not because their own needs do not have value to them, but because peace has a higher value. When their values are tapped into, they are motivated to action.

Motivating through manipulations such as guilting, withdrawing, whining and anger may get you an action you are looking for, but such manipulations won't reward you with a feeling of love. Remember, NLP has discovered that when the mind is given better options, it will choose a better option. Choosing positive motivation to request your partner to meet your need by linking it to one of their values is that better option.

I have already shared a few stories with you to show you this option in action. Now let's turn your attention to identifying your specific partner's values. The values list you want to obtain is the one your partner is actually living by, not the one they profess through philosophical thought. So your task is to identify the list that matters. How can you best do that?

Here are some helpful ideas from Dr. Dimartini that will give you the clues you need:

- Look around their space, and see what objects they keep around them. Do you see notes, documents, pictures, or reading material on either business, spirituality, hobbies, or investments, for example? Do you see lots of family pictures, sporting equipment or the tools for specific hobbies?

- In a social setting, listen for what topics energize them. What topics do they really enjoy getting into, or what topics do they seem to always draw a conversation into? Is it work, status, sports, family, spiritual pursuits, a hobby, culture, nature, travel?
- Look at how they spend their time, and in reverse, how they don't spend their time. We always have the time to do what we truly value, and rarely find the time to do those things we don't value.
- Look at their style. Do they like to blend in or make a statement (what kind of statement)? Are they colorful, frilly, casual, designed, earthy, luxurious?
- Look at what they spend their money on. Is it on learning, cultural pursuits, travel, sports, family, style, status, a hobby, entertainment, food?

These are a few ideas to help you to begin to see and to tune into your partner in a way that benefits your ability to get your needs met with an unreserved yes.

Now your task is to come up with at least 7 items you know your partner values. Once you have this list, write them down on the left side of a piece of paper. Then, think about all the needs you would like your partner to meet, and write these on the right side of the line you drew down the paper. Lastly, look at the list on the left and ask yourself this question:

"Which value of my partner's on the left can be linked to one of my needs on the right such that, by meeting my need, it fulfills my partner's value?"

Go back and re-read the three stories I gave you if you need help in seeing how to put the two together.

Try this for just one small need, then go practice it on your partner, and see how successful your results are. Since success builds upon success, once you master it on one small need, then increase your skill by practicing it on something a little more important.

As you begin to get less resistance and less compromise, notice how you can just sit back and watch your relationship symptoms begin to change automatically. How priceless is *that*?

For more help obtaining this critically important values list, you and your partner could take the test at

https://drdemartini.com/values/login

CHAPTER 18
VALUE SETS ARE INDIVIDUAL

In order to help you understand your partner's values, many relationship books will put you and your partner into two different groups, such a *Men Are From Mars Women Are From Venus*. In hypnotherapy school, I was also taught a 2-group theory, only this division was based on physical and emotional defense mechanisms.

Whatever the theory, how they help you is by letting you know that your partner is not as abnormal as you may think. The behavior for each partner-group is mapped on a bell curve of normality. The bell curve of male behavior, for example, only overlaps the bell curve for female behavior at its fringes, I would dare to say. However, people tend to think that behavior that is more than a couple standard deviations from their own group's normal behavior is abnormal. If this is how your brain thinks, then you will spend your time complaining. And complaining is a very quick way to grow and expand your negative view of your partner, ultimately driving wedges of discontent into your happy relationship.

What these theories teach is that each group is in fact perfectly normal – but on their own bell curve. Once you agree that your partner is normal, the hope is that you will then stop trying to change him or her into normal by *your* group's standard. And instead, you will start to find the tools to communicate between the two groups. This is healing and helps partners coexist more peacefully.

This is a great way to gain an improved perspective, but how often is it that neither you nor your partner quite fit within these individual group norms to start with?

When using a framework based on values, though, there is no group norm. Why is that? Because there is only one person in each group.

Why? Because no two people have the exact same set of values.
Value sets are as individual and unique as people are.

When you understand this, you can throw out all the books. You
can throw out a dozen techniques you could train yourself on. All you
simply need is

- to get curious and
- to pay attention.

Anyone can do this. You can just stop, look, and listen. How
simple is that? Now I am not saying that it doesn't take practice. That
it does take. Most of us are not that adept at stopping, looking, and
listening – or even being curious, for that matter. But with practice
comes progress. And with progress comes seeing. And seeing is
intoxicating – both to the seer and the one being seen.

Intoxication is your immediate gain. But quality communication to
get your needs met that actually works to build you a long-term
relationship is your real payoff. And isn't that a priceless use of your
energy and your time!

CHAPTER 19
EVERYONE WINNING HAS EVEN MORE BENEFITS

So to sum up, the second essential practice to learn (*after* you have practiced practiced practiced successfully using love languages to create your secure love bond) is one that allows you to express your concerns and your desires, your needs – but in such a way that does not alienate your partner – and becomes a **win-win** for both of you.

This practice centers on understanding and speaking within your partner's values. Since *"the only reasonable expectation you can have of people is that they will live according to their values"*, as Dr. John Demartini shares in his book, then

connecting your needs to your partner's values is a simple way to create a desire, from the heart,

to join you in your need.

This little-known piece of knowledge narrows your task down to mastering just one practice. You can use this one practice to create a communication within your relationship that actually works to inspire positive responses when asking for your needs to be met.

Yet it also has a secondary gain.

When someone recognizes your values, and speaks to you in terms of your values, it lights up your interest.

Have you ever been at a party, feeling a bit bored and tired, and then someone starts talking to you about something you value, like business or sports or family or travel or spirituality or a hobby? What happens? Don't you kind of wake up, and feel interested again, happy, eager?

67

The same happens in reverse when you start looking for your partner's values and you learn to speak your needs in terms of them. They feel seen; they feel heard. They become eager, lean in, get interested.

With these two gains to be had, how priceless could it be for you to master this practice?

PRACTICE #3

MENDING VS. DEFENDING

CHAPTER 20
TRAUMAS & DRAMAS

So far, you have gained the knowledge that to build a relationship that works, helping your partner to *feel* **loved, not just** *be* **loved**, will allow a multitude of annoyances to go unseen. And a **win-win** strategy for asking for your needs to be met will eliminate the day-to-day sacrifices that drive wedges of resentment over time into your love bond. If you apply just these two practices daily, you'll be able to sit back and just watch the shift in your relationships as they begin to take on a positive glow. Practice always brings progress.

These two practices are amazing cornerstones for building relationships that you will love to be in love with. And if you master even one of these practices, you will have gained so much more peace and happiness.

Yet, there is still one more fundamental cornerstone that underlies a relationship that has the power to resolve most anything that comes up. Triggers. Triggers, based on old wounds, will still invade your happy relationship. How you handle those triggers can draw you and your partner closer together – or drive wedges of misunderstandings, that result in feelings of not being seen nor heard, into your little paradise.

It wasn't until I was taught about the developmental traumas while working on my counseling certification that I found the best practice for this third underlying problem.

I call this problem *traumas and dramas*. This is where you end up in those escalating battles with your partner, each of you trying to pull the other to your own mindset, wondering why your partner doesn't see how what you are saying is so obvious. You look at your partner dumbfounded that they could be so (you can fill in the blank). From your perspective, what your partner is saying or doing is incomprehensible. You cannot understand why they are responding the way they are. You might angrily look at them and say, *"What the f...! All I said was ...! Why are you ...? Why don't you grow up!"* And then you get into a head-to-head argument – because nothing is making sense, and nothing your partner is saying is clarifying it. Your partner doesn't even get why he or she is being so (you can fill in the blank). So they get defensive, respond with hurt and anger and guilt, and you could potentially end up in an emotional fight you both regret.

When this happens, what you are encountering is one of your partner's **defenses**. We all have them. You too. Most of these defenses go all the way back to the developmental years – so far back that neither of you even know why you respond the way you do sometimes. Neither of you can explain it. Both of you get triggered, and all either of you can do is react. It doesn't make sense, and doesn't it seem like it never will?

To understand this, let's look at how defenses get started. From conception through puberty, there are 5 developmental stages. Each stage is susceptible to a specific trauma common to everyone, to varying degrees. Usually, though, one of these 5 basic traumas will resonate the most with each person. These 5 development traumas breed 5 basic defensive walls that serve to protect and keep safe during a time when our minds are too young and inexperienced to do otherwise.

Let's apply this to your partner. When the vulnerable emotions that your partner guarded with their defenses during these 5 stages, remain unresolved, these defenses will carry into their adult life, where, unbeknownst to them and you, they wreak havoc when triggered. These defenses were at one time very helpful, but now, no longer serve your partner. When a trigger happens that activates their earlier unresolved vulnerability, they will act out according to the age they were when the defense was created. No wonder their responses don't appeal to your adult mind! And vice versa for them, by the way.

Practice #3: Mending VS. Defending

By learning about these:

- common defensive walls your partner created as a kid,
- the shame their child's mind believed in and hid behind those walls,
- and the connection those early traumas have to their adult dramas,

you have the opportunity to see behind their curtain. You have the opportunity to see the real intentions underlying their reactions to you. With this insight, you can drop any false stories you are wrapping around their behavior. You can also stop wondering, *"Why are they acting this way?"* And you can respond with more enlightened remarks than, *"This is stupid! Grow up!"* or *"There must be something wrong with you. I would never do/say that!"*

"When you know better, you do better," as Oprah often reminds us. With an understanding of what's behind the curtain, it's easier to understand your partner's responses when triggered. More options then taking it personally, and being triggered yourself, are available to you. Instead of escalating into blaming and shaming, you can watch your old frustrated reactions change into curiosity and compassion. Wondering more about the need for safety that is being triggered behind your partner's wall can become commonplace.

Does anyone need to be convinced that fighting drains your relationships and leaves you feeling misunderstood, unseen, unheard, and eventually wondering why the heck you're even in the relationship?

CHAPTER 21
HEALING AND MANAGING

When your partner tells you that you are pushing their buttons, a more accurate response would be for them to say that there is something old and unhealed inside that is being triggered by what you are saying or doing. The problem is not you, the button-pusher. The problem is the unhealed memory inside of your partner. The same goes for you when you tell your partner they are pushing your buttons.

Maybe not all, but most triggers you encounter can be attached to one of the 5 core traumas that happen to all children during their developmental years. If you learn the trauma associated with a particular trigger that is being reacted to, you have a choice to respond with curiosity, without taking it personally. And then you can identify the best response for managing it.

But let me say here, managing triggers will add more peace to your life than anything else I know of. This in turn will naturally increase the longevity of your relationships. But actually healing from traumas and letting them go, so that the trigger is no longer a part of you or your partner's life, will add joy. It is by far the better path for the long term.

However, as a Zen book I once read said, *"We cannot wait for the philosophers of life to unravel the mysteries of life. In the meantime, live we must."* That is to say, if you wait for you or your partner to become healed from all your traumas, you'll miss out on the day-to-day life that you must live in the meantime. So you need to do both – heal for the long run, and manage for the short run.

Healing early traumas is not the goal of this book. That would take a lot more pages, and overly complicate the simplicity I am trying to gift you here. However, when you can at least recognize that

74

something else is manipulating behind the curtain of your partner's words, then you can choose to get curious, and manage the situation instead of getting angry back. And how about doing the same for yourself, getting curious about your own triggers?

Does anyone need to be convinced that therein lays an opportunity for peace and healing?

CHAPTER 22
LET'S TALK DEFENSES

When a previous, *unresolved* event, still lodged in your partner's memory, gets triggered, your partner will defend his/herself with the same defense they created way back when the memory happened. This is completely normal, natural, and common to everyone. The defense was originally created for protection because, as an infant or child, your partner felt vulnerable, unsafe.

Back when your partner felt unsafe as a child, it was common for them to disassociate in some way. One way they could have disassociated was to leave their body, so to speak, and "space out", finding solace in their higher mental or spiritual planes. Another way could have been to collapse inwardly and give up, turning their attention to meeting other people's needs in hopes they would get the same back. Another way could have been to withdraw into a made-up world deep inside where no one could touch them. Another way could have been to fight back and push their will onto the world around them. And still another way could have been to control and perfect the world around them by organizing it into rigid patterns. These were all the common ways their child's mind would have adapted to their perceived need for safety. As an infant and child, they were too small, too young, and had no control. So with their defenses, they loved and cared for themselves in the only healthy way they could at that age.

All of this is true for you too.

However, carrying these defenses into their adulthood leads to projecting past traumas onto current situations – erroneously – and that, in turn, leads to confusion. You, as the receiver of such a projection, can be taken by surprise, not understand what just happened, and could most likely react in some way that escalates the situation into anger and hurt by bringing your own defense into the picture. Then, both you and your partner, begin to feel misunderstood, unloved, shamed and alienated. The result? Anger and frustration.

What happens when you get enough of this reaction? Don't you start cautioning yourself that it's better to *bite your tongue* or to *pick your battles*? Or perhaps you just stop listening and start absentmindedly agreeing? When these tactics are the best practice you have, sure they will provide more peace than not doing them. But the side effect is a belief that you can't talk openly and receptively with your partner. And that is sure way to erode trust. When mistrust starts to seep into your happy relationship, the excitement of your new love will begin to fade.

Yet, it is worth asking once again, *is this really necessary*? What if you could see behind the curtain of your partner's reactions? How much curiosity and compassion do you think would fill the place where anger and frustration used to be?

If your partner could see past your reactions, how much more would *you* feel seen and heard?

And what if you both mended vs defended when the other was triggered? How much more peace and trust would fill your relationship?

CHAPTER 23
THERE'S GOT TO BE A BETTER WAY!

As an adult, a lack of safety is better addressed through open, positive communication than through defending. If you could

- learn to recognize your partner's attacks as a normal result of their defenses,
- and these defenses as a normal result of their early childhood traumas,

you could react more often with curiosity instead of frustration. With curiosity, you could question what the need is for safety hidden behind your partner's defensive wall. And then you could help them by utilizing the best techniques for that defense. Isn't it easy to see how this could de-escalate what would otherwise escalate into an unresolved conflict?

With such a skill, you could also help your partner understand *your* defenses. By sharing your knowledge, you could help prevent them from getting upset with you because of the stories they also wrap around *your* behavior. How could that benefit you?

Take my situation as an example. At one time, my partner was interpreting my forgetfulness as a lack of caring for his need for safety. This angered him. Knowing that this wasn't true, I would get offended, and an argument would escalate. Unknown to me, my "carelessness" was triggering his defense known as the *trust defense*. (I'll explain the defenses later.) In response, his accusations were triggering my defense known as the *connection defense* (which I will also explain later). But once I learned why I was an "airhead" at times, I was able to communicate my source trauma and its resultant adult drama. To my amazement, he understood, and he stopped taking it as an affront to him personally. When understanding replaced the inaccurate story he was wrapping around my behavior, cooperation was the result. Instead of angrily yelling at me about I how I didn't care, he helped me find better options for remembering. Conflict resolved! We haven't fought about this since! Even if I occasionally slip up and absentmindedly ignore my prompts, he knows it's not because I don't care. So he doesn't take it personally anymore.

Before this better solution, the picture was one of two people talking to the wall of each other's defense, with both of us tucked safely behind our own wall -- neither of us was talking to the other, but rather at each other's walls. Is it any wonder confusion and anger escalated?

When my partner wrapped the story of me not caring around my actions, an angry energy surged through his body. To release it, he slung angry words at me. In return, my *connection defense* would get triggered, and I would feel indignant about being accused of not caring. With my need for connection wounded, I would lash out in anger also. Sound familiar?

Neither of us was getting the feedback we wanted because we were both defending vs. mending. Our reactions to each other were defensive, not curious. Reacting defensively left both of us feeling misunderstood and angry. Rather than escalate into a full on war, we would turn our backs on each other. We would stay this way until the anger dissipated, we felt sorry, and apologized – until the next time, of course.

But once I understood his *trust defense* and his own need for safety, I explained it to him, and I shared the best practice for managing it. In his case, the best practice was not to discuss it for at least 20 minutes, a waiting period for his angry energy to dissipate. I found that when I did this very simple thing, our discussions became less heated, and we were able to find positive resolutions for his need too. My need for connection, created by my *connection defense*, was left undisturbed, and instead of lashing back at him with indignant anger, our two needs shook hands with each other in cooperation.

In this book, you will discover the 5 common defenses (two of which I've casually mentioned already) and the most efficient responses to soothe each of those defenses. For now, I just wanted to whet your appetite with an example that showed how identifying the right defense and the right response to manage it can completely change the dynamic of a conflict and keep it from boiling over into a fight.

When you end a fight with unresolved anger, hurt or feeling misunderstood, it ripples out way past your relationship. You'll be curter with the world around you, less connected, more punishing to those that weren't even involved. So what I want for you and your partner is to avoid those hurtful arguments that make you feel misunderstood, indignant and angry. I want you to be truthfully happy, so that you treat your world to happy eyes and a warm smile. Your loving energy is important to everyone's happiness. Can you imagine, if we all knew how to manage our defenses better, how much more peace we could ripple around the world?

CHAPTER 24
THE 5 DEVELOPMENTAL DEFENSES

Any defense being triggered in your partner is a safety-cover layered over an insecure feeling of vulnerability. When you focus on the defensive *reactions* being used by their defense, the result is an endless loop of misunderstanding and hurt feelings.

So let's try something new! Instead of putting attention on the defense's reactions, how about refocusing your attention onto the *vulnerability* hiding behind the defense's wall? How could that change the outcome?

Let's see how this might work for you.

There are 5 stages of development your partner went through from birth to puberty. Because of the specific developmental growth that goes on in each of these stages, a particular need is also present in each. Here is a list of the 5 needs that correlate to the 5 developmental stages:

1. The Need For Connection, to be present
2. The Need To Be Nurtured, to feel full and satisfied
3. The Need For Self-Direction, to feel autonomous
4. The Need For Trust, to know others care
5. The Need To Be Accepted, to feel included

To reiterate, if your partner's need was not met in any one of these stages, they experienced that lack as a trauma. Their traumas resulted in a feeling of vulnerability. Their vulnerability resulted in a need to be protected. This protection showed up in the form of a defense.

As an adult, an action or word activates a memory tied to one of their un-resolved traumas. The defense for that trauma is then triggered, resulting in a drama with you that ends with hurt feelings, misunderstandings and alienation paining your love life.

Once you begin to understand these dynamics behind your arguments, you have more choices. You no longer need to become frustrated, offended, indignant or angry yourself. You have the opportunity to react with curiosity, and ask yourself, *"What is the need for safety behind this curtain?"* Curiosity will **de**-escalate any argument.

In the upcoming chapters, you will discover the key factors behind your partner's defenses so you can

- better understand the fears and shame their inner child is suffering from,
- know when you're talking to their wall of defense and not your beautiful partner tucked safely behind that wall,
- help to de-escalate and manage the defense better,
- develop a communication skill that will bring you both closer together that you can ripple out into all of your relationships.

A wonderful side note is you'll begin to see how those wounds developed some amazing gifts that your partner also carried into their adult life. Many people, when confronted with the choice of reliving their life without their traumas and thus giving up the wonderful character qualities that accompany the trauma say they would rather keep the traumas.

And here's the best part of all: You can also apply all of this to yourself.

CHAPTER 25
THE GIFTS OF THE WOUND

No one gets through childhood unscathed by a trauma or two. But in every dark cloud, there is a silver lining. In every wound, there is a gift. Focusing on the gift vs the wound can make the difference between resistance and acceptance. In resistance is pain. In acceptance, appreciation can be found; happiness can be found.

If you focus your attention on what you lost, then anger, self-pity, resentment and lashing out is the cost. And have you ever seen a happy person with those seething in their heart? But if you focus on what was gained, then gratitude can be your result. You (and your partner) can look back on your traumas and say, *"Thank you! I am what I am today; I have certain gifts in my life today **because** I went through that event!! And for **that** result, I **can** be grateful."*

The trauma happened; there is no changing that. And it was undeserved; there's no changing that. Yet if looking back is on what was gained (and there is definitely a silver lining in every dark cloud), appreciation and joy can fill your heart instead of resentment. When you choose to fill your heart with resentment, you choose unhappiness. When you choose to fill your heart with appreciation, you choose happiness. It's your choice, and all you have to do is say yes.

Stop for a moment, and breathe that in, please.

Let's look at your own character qualities or skills or connections. Which ones came out of traumas you suffered? Are you more compassionate? Are you more empathetic to others, more capable of helping? Are you more determined? Did you develop a sense of humor to lighten situations? Did you gain a specific skill set? Did you get an opportunity to connect with someone or something that you may not have otherwise? Are any, or all of these, a result of, and thus a beautiful gift of, a trauma that you underwent?

I remember a daughter beating her father up about leaving the family. Rather than getting apologetic, this enlightened dad redirected her attention to what she gained. He asked her how much she loved horseback riding. It was her biggest love. He then asked her whether she thought she would be involved in riding had she not met her step father. He then pointed out that she still had her father's attention, just not daily in the home. And now that she has 2 fathers, her life has been enriched with a hobby she would never want to give up.

In my own life, as another example, I trace my writing ability back to an early trauma. By the time I was 8 or 9, I was isolated in my room, no longer a part of my family. I wasn't allowed friends, or school social events. To avoid my stepmother, I began to live alone in my room, coming out to clean, cook and go to school only. It seemed I could do no right in her eyes.

Around then, I developed a speech impediment called a lateral lisp (think Daffy Duck). So the schools I attended kept sending me to speech therapists. Although I was quiet and withdrawn, one therapist, in my junior high years, could just look at me and see how distraught I was. I was too insecure to feel safe speaking about it with him. On the few occasions I had tried to talk to an adult, it had backfired on me, and no help had ever come from those single moments of courage. However, this adult did not stop when I just looked at the floor and said nothing. If he couldn't get me to open up, he suggested I write in a notebook and gave me one. That simple gesture of kindness was a life saver. I was able to express onto those pages all my pent up emotions lurking under my docile exterior. This channeling of my emotions most likely saved me from becoming an angry and frustrated adult who lashed out at the world for not feeling loved enough.

What were the gifts? I learned a constructive way to release and process my emotions. I also developed writing skills. I became obsessed with doing well in school (because teachers gave me the attention I yearned for at home). In high school, one teacher even had me grade her literature papers.

What character qualities can I attribute directly to suffering as an outcast in my family? I dropped down out of my analytical mind and added heart, compassion and empathy that I believe I would not have otherwise. I now know how to listen attentively and to nurture. At an early age, I began asking why about everything. Thus I'm an independent thinker, who rarely follows the normal thoughts of the masses. I began to read psychology at the age of 12. By the time I was 14, I was an excellent problem solver. I also had to learn discernment, and gained a high attention to details and body language. And of course, I have a fierce need for freedom. That's good because I am very tolerant of another's right to live and let live, and to be exactly who they are, and not wrap my own stories around their behavior.

If I could go back and relive my childhood without the trauma, but had to give up all these skills and gifts to do so, would I? Absolutely NOT! That's all in the past now. I love owning these gifts. And now that I'm no longer in that situation, I can use them and create the life I want to live. So why not keep them and focus my energy on what I CAN do?

So as you proceed and discover more about the traumas and dramas in the chapters that follow, I invite you to keep in mind:

with every trauma, great gifts are *also* born.

As you read through each of the early developmental stages, I will end each one with a list of beautiful gifts that could be developed *because* of the trauma common to that stage. Highlighting and focusing on the *gift* in a wound is critically important to utilizing this knowledge to its best effect. Can you see how helpful that is?

85

CHAPTER 26
THE KEY TO HAPPINESS

There is one more thing I want to address before you begin your encounter with the 5 defenses in the next chapter. I want to take a moment to give you the key to happiness.

To be happy only requires that you to give up 2 things:

- criticism
- and fear.

These two things create an energy in your life that *"cramps your style"*, so to speak, weighs you down, and drains your ability to create. Negativity towards the world and others, like your partner, is like taking poison and expecting the other person to die.

To *give up* something, though, does not mean to grit your teeth and bear it. That's the dishonest way of giving it up because that's pretense, isn't it? No, to give up something, you have to honestly *let it go*, don't you? So how do you let go of criticism and fear? It turns out, this too is quite simple: you simply look beyond it to something behind it. That's a technique we have been discussing for the last few chapters.

Let's see how this works to release criticism, as fear will follow a similar pattern.

To give up criticism, you need but look past the outward behavior to the truth behind that behavior. How is that done? Well, how many times have you heard someone defend a friend with something like, *"I know what you mean, but you don't know him the way I do. If you only knew ... "*? Or how many times have you judged a person's behavior – only to find out you were missing pieces of intention that, once known, changed your judgment into compassion?

For example, I was in hypnotherapy school when this lesson struck

86

home for me. John Kappas, during the years when he began his Hypnosis Motivational Institute, gave free sessions to individuals who agreed to be taped for his student's education.

On one tape, a man came in, whose story I do not recall. But I do vividly recall my reaction to him. I thought of him as so reprehensible that he deserved to be run through a wood chipper – alive, feet first. Can you imagine my surprise when only 15 minutes later, after listening to John peel back the layers of this person's life, I completely changed my reaction to one of compassion!

What an eye-opener that was for me! In only 15 minutes, I went from feeling justified in torturing this man, did a 180-degree turn, and came out on the other side with a feeling of compassion. And all it took was seeing the sadness locked in this man's frozen heart over years and years of events that caused him pain. Now, decades later, he was a hardened and abusive adult. And I wondered – if I had the same experiences in my life, could I not be an abusive adult too?

This experience matured me and changed forever how I listened to other people and how I responded to what I heard. I found that I began to delve into the undercurrents in their stories, and I began to see the higher intentions they were trying to fulfill with their behavior. Interestingly, I then discovered the same result again and again: people were not as mean as they looked by their outward behavior at all. What began to evolve for me was the understanding that all negative outward behavior was nothing more than a cry for help. It was a lashing out at the world for not feeling loved enough. Yes, I fully understood that negative behavior needed to be contained or managed -- because it hurts others. But was that a reason for me to look down on or despise the person who was hurting underneath all that negativity?

You see, unity is a part of our spiritual DNA. Peace can only be obtained in a spirit of unity. Separation and isolation are ABnormal behavior. They are a defense used to protect ourselves from the stories we tell ourselves about other people's behavior.

For me, now whenever I look past such behavior to the truth hidden behind the curtain, I do not take it personally – because I can see that it has nothing to do with me. Yes, I notice that I can say or do something that triggers the wound in another, and then feel attacked as the wound reacts. But the cause truly has nothing to do with me.

To bring this idea into your life, if you deal with the attack instead of the cause, don't you just cycle through the outlash again and again and again? And doesn't this in turn wound you, and result in alienation? And then, don't you begin to separate yourself, leading to your own sense of loneliness and isolation? So who pays a real cost here?

What would happen if you didn't take it personally? Instead of reacting to your partner's attack, what would happen if you looked at it with curiosity, wondering what the true cause was? What if you peeled back the layers instead, and saw the old unresolved pain that was being triggered, as I did with that reprehensible man in my hypnosis class?

What would happen if someone did that for you? What would happen if you did it for yourself?

How much criticism would begin to fade away in your thoughts? How much unity could you re-establish? How much longer could your relationships last and how much more comforting would your bond feel? And with comfortable bonds, how much more at peace would you be? How much happiness could you create for yourself and your partner?

The quality of your life is closely based on the quality of the questions you ask yourself. So how much benefit could you obtain if you took a moment out from your reading, and pondered the answers to all these questions for yourself.

Looking past, in short, is nothing more than giving yourself a new perspective. Perspective truly *IS* everything. The perspectives you have are nothing more than stories you tell yourself. Tell yourself a different story, and you change your perspective. Change your perspective, and you change your feelings. Change your feelings, and you change the quality of your life.

You must learn to forgive, not because you are being "good" and "charitable", but because what you are seeing, the story of meanness and evil you are telling yourself, is simply not true. And in this way, you not only help to heal others from their unresolved traumas being expressed in their behavior, you gift *yourself* unity, peace and happiness.

NOW let's tackle the defenses – keeping in mind the importance of changing perspectives and of the gifts each wound also gives.

CHAPTER 27
DEFENSE #1
FOR THE NEED FOR CONNECTION

What Is The Defense And Its Underlying Trauma?

In this stage, when a child comes from abuse in another life, or suffers birth trauma, or is an unwanted baby, or lacks a strong connection to its mother, it experiences its new body as "*I just got here, and already things are going wrong!*" It then believes the world is a dangerous and terrifying place. In defense, it discovers protection in not being fully present in its body.

These children grow into adults who lack connection with their bodies. They have difficulty staying present and easily wander off in thought. They have not felt safe in the world from birth, or even before; therefore, deeply ingrained in their subconscious, the world is terrifying. They may have been born into an unsafe environment such as a war zone. Perhaps they had physical problems while being born. Or maybe mommy was not able to give them enough touching and eye contact to help them feel secure in the world. In any case, this defense lives with a deep-seeded fear that the world is not safe and they do not have the right to exist. Thus they grow up with an existential fear of life itself, and that being alive is somehow shameful.

What Adult Dramas Does This Defense Produce?

This defense breeds adults who have difficulty staying connected. They may be referred to as daydreamers, scattered, spacey, forgetful, airheads, or an absent-minded professor.

They walk around in what seems like a cloud and can be forgetful because they are lost in thought. Their bodies or their vehicles may be bruised from running into things. Their clothes may even be unique or disheveled, like Einstein.

They find it easier to connect to the universe of ideas or the universe of the spirit, but less easy to connect to humans. Those high in this defense can even be afraid of people, withdrawn, not wanting a lot of contact from others. The world of the mind or spirit is typically more important than this mundane life and its worldly interactions with people. They favor animals, art or a solitary activity over activities with people.

They tend to focus more on intelligence and logic, and less on feeling. They use their will and mind to engage with others. Some could even have contempt for those they see as emotional. They could also be prideful about their intelligence or their spirituality (but do so only out of a need to feel some sense of control).

Many have a sense of being outside of themselves at times, watching themselves and the world from a disassociated perspective, with a matter-of-fact attitude. Often they will believe they do not belong in the world, they don't fit in, they must be "from another planet" or another time, a visitor on the outside looking in.

They can be quick to jump into intellectualizing and analyzing when uncomfortable events and situations arise. This is their way of disassociating from the feelings that arise.

They often feel more comfortable and confident interacting with people when living within a role (mother, teacher, doctor, student, hobbyist, businessman, etc.) as this gives them control and guidelines for interaction.

For those that are high in this defense, they often read anger and attack into other people's looks and comments, telling themselves negative things that others think about them. This can lead them to reject before being rejected.

When they say, "*I can do it myself*," they are often projecting their feeling of being a burden to others or of being inadequate.

It's not uncommon to hear them speak of their belief in the meaninglessness of life.

They are very sensitive to pain – to their own and to other's.

Since they are not enclosed by their body, they have weak boundaries. Therefore, if they don't adopt a framework or a role within which to navigate the world, they will be overly sensitive to stepping out into the world. This shows up as anxious, nervous, or edgy in unknown environments where they have no sense of control.

Their world could even be so overwhelming to them that they fragment and fall apart. For many, environmental stimulus can be too much; they can be bothered by sounds and disorganization. Sloppiness and lack of neatness and order can trigger deep, underlying feelings of chaos.

It's common for them to have sensitivities or allergies to foods or to the environment. Their bodies tend towards dryness and brittleness. Their muscles tend to be tight in their upper body, even when lying down.

They are often characterized as an airhead, a talking head or a nerd in the media.

They use sex to feel alive, and to obtain connection.

What Are Best Practices For Managing This Defense?

These adults need to feel secure, understood, connected. Move slowly with them, no surprises. Always tell them what's going on.

If the spacey, absent-minded airhead shows up in your partner, what they need most is to get grounded, and not to be made fun of. Help them get out of their head (where they escape) and into their body. For example, ask them to focus on a few deep breaths, slow down their speech, and use their inner sight, like a flashlight, and locate the feeling in their body. Putting your hand on their forearm at the same time will draw their attention downward too.

Other ways that help them feel grounded, more centered, and less spacey are relaxing in a warm bath, a foot massage, shuffling their feet on the ground, walking barefoot in the grass, focusing their thoughts on their energy flowing down into their legs and feet, to name a few.

If they start disassociating, talking too fast, and intellectualizing, place your hand firmly on their forearm, give them solid and gentle eye contact, and smile sincerely. Mention that you notice their speech speeding up. Tell them you are really interested in hearing what they are saying, and ask them if they would be willing to take a couple deep breaths and slow down so you can follow them better. This will help them feel the warmth of safe, open contact, and your enjoyment of them so they don't fall into negative self-criticism.

Sometimes it just takes acknowledging the space needs to change, like going to another restaurant or moving to a different table.

If they get anxious, they can regulate by rocking and/or panting in through the nose and out through the mouth. Containment and creating a boundary helps them too, like wrapping in a blanket or a shawl, or getting into a cozy small space. Some like the feeling of being compressed – like a heavy blanket, or a bear hug or having a partner lay on them for a few moments.

What Are Some Of The Gifts Born From This Wound?

High intelligence
Spiritual connection, access to higher consciousness
Curious mind, loves to soak in information
Avant guard creativity, good imagination
Unique perspectives on life, precious insights
Inspires with visions of possible realities (think Einstein)
Dry wit, intelligent humor (think Woody Allen)

Compassion, empathy, sensitivity to pain – for self and others
Low tolerance for violence
Love of nature, animals, gardening and wanting to protect
Independence
Spontaneity

CHAPTER 28
DEFENSE #2
FOR THE NEED TO BE NURTURED

What Is The Defense And Its Underlying Trauma?

In this stage, when a child's needs are consistently not met, its experience is that *"there is not enough; I am not enough"*. It then believes that the world is a place of lack, that enough does not exist to feel full and be completely satisfied. Such lack can be centered on bodily needs, like food, or on emotional needs, like attention. In defense, it discovers protection in collapsing and giving up.

These children grow into adults who have lost touch with their own needs. Therefore, they have difficulty receiving nurturance. Deeply ingrained in their subconscious mind is a belief that others really don't want to give to them. Perhaps mommy was incapable of giving milk, or hurried while feeding, not giving her baby enough time to be satiated on its own. Perhaps mommy was too young, or a single parent, or overwhelmed with too many responsibilities or other children. In any case, this defense lives with a deep persistent sense of emptiness, of always being in want, never satiated, never full, and that having needs is somehow selfish and shameful.

What Adult Dramas Does This Defense Produce?

This defense breeds adults who struggle to uncover who they are and how they fit into society. They readily put blame on how they were treated. They desperately want to be included, and may create a scene or be overly fussy merely to gain the attention they crave. This craving can come across as clingy or as artificial. The artificial mask is an attempt to adapt to what they think people want to see in order to include them.

Although they desperately want others to *want* to pay attention to them, they often have difficulty receiving it gracefully and can feel awkward about it as they debate inside of their mind whether or not the other person is sincere. When they do take it in, like a loving puppy, they will attach themselves and follow that person anywhere.

Since they resigned themselves to their own needs being unfulfilled, they find it easier to attune to the needs of other's than their own. Poking into other's business satisfies a need to be included. Taking in other people's stories gives them a sense of fullness. So they love to chat and listen to other's stories.

They tend to be caregivers, and rescue others in an attempt to feel like they matter, that they are important in another's life. Some even experience anxiety when they are incapable of meeting a request. At the same time, they can also feel taken advantage of, not having a sense of when to say no. *"Do a little bit more each day than everyone expects, and soon everyone expects more"* must have been written by someone in this defense. Therefore, they can vacillate between appearing self-centered and being a rescuer.

When feeling left out, they often state that they don't need anything from anyone, or that they do everything for themselves, and sadly collapse into an attitude of, *"Oh, no, don't bother about me. I'm ok with being left out"*. Yet, if put on the spot, they could be so dissociated from their own needs, and so busy taking care of other's needs, that they don't even know what they truly want anymore.

They will compare themselves to others, be envious of what others have, and, if willing to express outwardly, make comments on how others could be willing to give them more, and want to do more for them.

When they do seek for a need to be met, they could be overt, demanding and justifying their right. Or they could be covert, implying that if you don't do it, you will be made to feel guilty or wrong in some way. Of all the defenses, they are the most likely to attempt to survive via manipulating others into giving with the use of such tools as guilt, blame, justification, and especially whining.

It's common for their self-talk to say that they are the ones who must conform and give-in in order to be accepted. At the same time they can be pouty that their needs are not considered, wondering why they are always left out, not good enough or loved enough. This triggers their shame, so it's common for them to cover their true image with a "more acceptable" mask to the public.

They have serious self-worth issues, but often hide behind an exterior wall of pride.

They have a high degree of body awareness, are highly concerned about how their physical appearance comes across to others, and tend to use physical appearance to attract others.

Addictions are common, as well as anxiety or even panic attacks.

Issues around food are common, as are digestive problems. They are often quite picky and fussy – especially about food and/or about how people relate to them. Things are just never quite good enough because they are actually projecting their own deep sense of not being good enough. Some can even acquire a "high maintenance" label.

When not feeling loved, they tend towards gossip that picks on others. Lowering others is way to make themselves seem less low.

They are usually quite chatty, and go off on tangents and stories. Being good talkers, they quite often out-talk their own therapists.

They have a need for others to make them feel better, and can come across to others as needy or clingy, and are often characterized as so in the media.

They use sex to fill full. They give sex in order to get contact.

What Are Best Practices For Managing This Defense?

It would be useful to these adults to spend time figuring out what they truly like, what they truly want. All they know is that they want somebody to do something to show them they are appreciated and wanted. You could ask them to ponder the things that make them happy, and journal the list so they can share it with you and also remember it for themselves.

If your partner collapses into sadness about how much they give and give and give, but who gives back to them, what they need is to feel full. Give them your undivided attention. You could also have them sit between your legs with their back to your chest, wrap your arms around them, and just breathe at the same rate they do. Assure them they can collapse into the feeling of being held. Do this for at least 20 minutes.

The neediness of this defense makes being around them somewhat difficult for many people. This reaction reinforces in them that there is not enough love to go around, and increases their subconscious shame at having needs. Their way out of this needy image is to learn to make requests in such a way that doesn't alienate others. A useful communication tool to do this can be found in Marshall Rosenberg's book, *Nonviolent Communication*. Paraphrased, it gives us a 3-part structure that goes like this:

1. I feel (add feeling) when you (add objective behavior).
2. I have a need for (add need).
3. Would you be willing to (add request)?

Examples:

- *I feel abandoned when you walk away. I have a need to communicate. Would you be willing to give me 30 minutes to explain?*
- *I feel scared when you raise your voice. I have a need to feel safe. Would you be willing to take a breath and quietly respond?*

Practice #3: Mending VS. Defending

- *I feel so alone. I need some connection. Would you be willing to spend some quality time with me today?*

I was awed when I saw the results of this languaging when I was first taught it. The trick, or hack, that makes it work is to ensure the feeling phrase is a *feeling* and not a *judgment* about the other person's behavior. "*I feel you are using me, being disrespectful, or being a jerk*" are judgments, not feelings. These will not result in needs being met, but rather in resentment and resistance. A feeling pertains to oneself. Lists of feelings can be found on the internet.

Until your partner masters this, you could encourage their thoughts along this line. Try saying,

- *I hear that you are feeling ... when I ... Is that correct?*
- *What is it you need right now?*
- *Would you like to make a request?*

Another healthy way to make a request is what we discussed earlier in this book. Encourage your partner to review the section on linking their request to your value system to produce a win-win for both of you. This should be easy for this defense as they are naturally attuned to others.

Help your partner to notice the many ways their needs are met throughout their day by many people. Even a store-clerk's smile adds to their fullness if noticed and received.

Gifts must show that you care, that you LISTENED to them. They should be something that you heard them say they wanted or that can make their life easier.

What Are Some Of The Gifts Born From This Wound?

Compassion and empathy for others needs
Able to easily tune into other's needs
Nurturing, giving, generous
Good listeners (hearing other's stories fills them up)

How To Keep Your X's & O's From Becoming Exes & Woes

Good counselors
Natural teachers (can pace so student can swallow)
A gift for gab and telling stories
Enjoys meeting with others
Loyal (like when you adopt a lonely puppy)
Curious
Graceful
Natural innocence and sweetness
Charming
Capacity for delight and child-like pleasure

CHAPTER 29
DEFENSE #3
FOR THE NEED TO SELF DIRECT

What Is The Defense And Its Underlying Trauma?

In this stage, when a child's attempts at exploring and experiencing are smothered or shamed as it begins to individuate from mommy, its experience is that *"it's more important to please others than to please myself"*. It then believes that what it wants is not considered important by others. In defense, it submits to self-abandonment and enduring the invasion, outwardly complying. It discovers protection in shutting down and retreating, trying to be invisible.

These children grow into adults who have lost touch with what they think. They have difficulty speaking up and having a voice in disagreements. Deeply ingrained in their subconscious is a rebellion and rage against others telling them what they should do or think. Perhaps mommy could not handle her child's need for individuality, or wanted her child to be an extension of herself. Perhaps she was a *"helicopter parent"* that fussed over or worried about her child too much, preventing it from having a voice or to make its own choices. In any case, this defense lives with a deep-seeded fear of being invaded and losing their autonomy, and that being seen is somehow shameful.

What Adult Dramas Does This Defense Produce?

This defense breeds adults who feel a need to comply, take the blame, and endure the shame. They are outwardly compliant, yet inwardly defiant. Self-expression is bottled up, and they tend to withhold their voice and shut down in tense situations.

They are not always quick to know what they think, and therefore, may have a long response time, not seem to be responding at all, or answer, *"I don't know"* a lot.

When they do withdraw, they may not be "seen" for long periods of time. *"If you do that to me, I am going to get so quiet you can't find me. Something will change, but you won't know what it was, but you will know something is wrong, and I'm not going to tell you."*

They are easily invaded because of undeveloped boundaries, with a tendency to be overly sensitive to getting their feelings hurt.

They may ask for helpful advice when they need it, or ask what you think, but then turn around and respond to one idea after the next with how that simply couldn't work for them.

It is common for them to have an internal no to someone wanting them to be a certain way or to tell them anything, for no other reason than it is coming from outside of themselves. Therefore, they have a resistance to other people's ideas of what they should think, do, or be like.

They try not to stand out in a crowd, and try to fly under the radar.

They are passive aggressive. When they attack, it is usually sideways as confronting directly can be uncomfortable, but they *"are going to get you sooner or later"*. They may tell you something by telling someone else within your hearing range. I even had someone make a note on my retirement card, for all to read, that I didn't back them up on something that happened years before. If they do respond to you, they will often say that nothing is wrong, or that they are fine, yet ensure that their body language informs you that something is quite wrong. Or they may go down the path of *"Fine. It's all my fault. I'll take the blame."*

Some can be notorious mis-matchers, and have a talent for twisting something said or done into something not said or done. They may also egg you into blowing up, so they can make you look wrong.

Practice #3: Mending VS. Defending

Deep down, they feel if they succeed, it's as though their parent is winning. Therefore, often they will subconsciously choose unwise decisions that hurt themselves.

They are often characterized in the media as the disheartened wimp that doesn't stand up for themselves or the adult who walks away silently from an argument and retreats into another room.

They use sex to be seen.

They tend to pad and protect their sensitivity by being overweight, especially around the mid-section of their body.

What Are Best Practices For Managing This Defense?

What these adults need is to feel that they are in control of themselves, autonomous and that they have choice. If you keep pushing them, you will push them right out of your life. They also need **time** to process their own thoughts and know their own sense of self.

If your partner withdraws, becomes quiet, and retreats into hiding, let them go. Honor their right to come and go as they please. Be patient. If you corner them, push them, or say things like, *"Talk to me! Don't you walk away from me!"* they will experience that as being invaded. Also, don't rush them. They will be back when they are ready and when they know what they think. When they do come out, delight in it so they feel safe being seen by you.

This defense appreciates choices and being asked vs. told or advised. So avoid telling them what they should do, and instead make a request. If not, their rebellious streak may surface. Try giving just 2 choices. Questions like, *"Which do you prefer, this or that?"* or *"Would it be ok if we talked now or in an hour?"* allows them to feel their autonomy and speeds up the response time for you. Change the word *should* in all your sentences to the word *could* to allow your partner to experience your ideas as a choice.

If your partner has trouble speaking up, help them to find their own voice. Give them time to figure out their response to your queries, rather than hurrying them or finishing their sentences and thoughts for them. It may take them several minutes, or even days to discover what they think as they tend to look outside to what you want to hear vs. inside to what their own ideas are.

If a communication is vital, and your partner is having a difficult time speaking up, work with them on a physical gesture they can use that doesn't require words.

Show them that their thoughts and feelings have value. Remember that they interpreted their upbringing as though what they wanted didn't matter. So be sure to respond, and follow through, when they do make a request.

If your partner often answers "*I don't know*", try responding, "*I know you don't know, but if you did, what would you know or what would it be?*" This typically stimulates a response when someone is blocked.

If they sideswipe you, or attack you in an indirect way, just know there is a back-story in their mind that you may never know. As a necessary way of letting out their pent up emotions, on some deep level, hurting others feels good to this defense. Bear in mind that they were told no and their behavior was wrong way too much as a kid. If you keep your distance and don't engage with their defense, this will produce better results than blaming, shaming and making them wrong. Just say, "*Ouch!*" to show them that their words hurt, and meet the hurt with compassion, reminding them of their true gentleness of heart.

This defense has a suppressed inner anger that has been pushed down for a long time. This seethes below the surface as a rage that they are actually afraid of. It would be helpful to them to learn to identify the way the anger signals its presence -- before it explodes. For them, the signal may be a tiny ping inside or a small voice. It's best they don't wait for the ping or voice to get really loud in order to know that they are having a problem. Since they can take the blame, bear the shame, and just swallow it for a long time, when they do let it out, watch out. So be gentle with them. Give them enormous space and time to metabolize what they are feeling.

Since, as a child, they had no advocate, be their advocate that says, *"this will not happen on my watch"*. Rather than rolling your eyes, making fun of them, or shaming them in other people's eyes, defend them!

What Are Some Of The Gifts Born From This Wound?

Super gentle
Kind
Sweet
Loving and warm
Careful not to sound pushy
Patient
Caring
Sensitive and compassionate
A capacity to keep a secret
Great sense of humor
Patient
Perseverant and determined when they finally have a clear yes inside
Creative

CHAPTER 30
DEFENSE #4
FOR THE NEED TO TRUST

What Is The Defense And Its Underlying Trauma?

In this stage, when a child's attempts at finding its own power are dominated and put down by its parents, who strongly exert their own agenda, it experiences a power struggle. It then believes that "*the world is a battleground, and I have to be in control to be safe.*" In defense, it discovered protection by conquering its world through bullying or seduction.

These children grow into adults who have lost touch with their ability to believe in others; therefore, they have difficulty showing weakness, leaning on others or accepting that others are capable. Deeply ingrained in their subconscious is a need to control. Perhaps they had a volatile, controlling parent, whose desire for their child's life was the only acceptable path. Perhaps they had a parent that hit them, abusively punished them, or slung contemptuous words at them anytime they did not perform up to their parent's standards. Perhaps their parent was trying to live out their own lost dreams through their child's performance, and wanted their child to fulfill some physical or emotional need the parent had. Perhaps their parent felt threatened by their child's success, and couldn't bear for their child to be better than the parent. Perhaps their parent required them to grow up before they were capable. In any case, this defense has a deep-seeded fear of letting go and trusting, and that being vulnerable is a weakness that is somehow shameful.

What Adult Dramas Does This Defense Produce?

Practice #3: Mending VS. Defending

This defense breeds adults who are overly concerned about safety, aware of impending danger at all times, and who are the back seat drivers of other's lives. They have trouble trusting that others are aware and capable and believe they have to fight in order to be seen and heard. When they exert their control, it's through anger and bullying or through seduction and charm. They have a need to have it their way, therefore, are often referred to as bossy, and can seem intimidating and pushy.

Although they are *mentally* big and strong, they are *emotionally* very fragile. They have a deep insecurity about being abandoned, and are thus torn between their need for others to want them, and their need to control others to feel safe.

Since they carry a fear of people using or betraying them (from their childhood), trusting others with what they perceive as their weakness is difficult for them. When they decide they can trust, though, their loyalty has no boundaries.

They tend to have admiration for those they see as winners and contempt for those they see as losers.

They are often characterized as the bully or the seductive charmer in the media.

They use sex to either dominate or to expose themselves to vulnerability.

What Are Best Practices For Managing This Defense?

What these adults need most is to feel they can trust you. Never lie to them, even to save their feelings. Be up front about everything vs. letting them discover it.

If your partner hassles you over something you did that seems unsafe to them, respond to them with equal and opposite pressure. Do not back down, but also do not engage with their anger either. Instead, directly, calmly and firmly say that you love them and are not going anywhere (remember they fear abandonment), but that you are also not having this conversation at this moment. Give them at least 20 minutes for the energy to pass through their bodies and dissipate. Then sit down and calmly discuss their issue with you.

If the backseat driver shows up in your partner, thank them for caring, remind them that you are capable, and that a positive growth for them is to trust and allow.

If their bossiness begins to annoy you, keep in mind that their intention is your safety and well being. Help them learn to say words that don't sound so bossy. Shifting from negative action words (a command) to positive action words (a question) can make a big difference in how the thought is received by you. For example, *"don't forget"* can be changed to *"are you remembering"* or *"don't drop"* can be changed to *"are you holding"* or *"I need you to"* can be changed to *"would you be willing to"*. Another way for them to soften the bossiness of their sentences is to make a statement with the tonality of a question, with that little upturn at the end.

Because they are aggressive when angry, they may worry about their inner rage and fear hurting those they love. So they may choose to leave when they get triggered. In that case, let them go, and don't take it personally. They are super loyal and not abandoning you, but rather protecting you. After their angry energy dissipates, they should be able to discuss their problem calmly with you.

What Are Some Of The Gifts Born From This Wound?

Leadership, not afraid to carry the lead role
Loyal, devoted, will see it through
Passionate, can hold firm to what they believe
Willing to fearlessly stand in battle for a noble, worthy cause
Courage to stand for right
Protective

Practice #3: Mending VS. Defending

Advocates for the underdog, "knights in shiny armor"
Alert to impending danger, strong sense of safety awareness
Strategizes one step ahead to be ready to react
Clear headed and effective in crisis
"I can" attitude, will find a way to survive
Gets up and tries again
Not afraid of the world, can travel alone
Self confident, knows their value, stands even with others
Spontaneous
Sense of humor used to break up tension
Charismatic, charming, seductive
Gentlemanly or lady like

CHAPTER 31
DEFENSE #5
FOR THE NEED TO BE ACCEPTED

What Is The Defense And Its Underlying Trauma?

In this stage, when a child has its affections ignored, refused or embarrassed as it begins to discover its own body, its experience is that *"feelings are messy and out of control"*. It then believes that its own feelings are something to be stifled and hidden. In defense, it discovers protection in knowing the rules of what is expected, perfecting and organizing its world, and judging how to behave and respond appropriately.

These children grow into adults who confuse approval with love and have lost touch with their authentic reactions and emotions. They have difficulty accepting imperfection. Deeply ingrained in their subconscious is the idea that they have to be perfect, follow the rules and do everything right in order to be loved. Perhaps their parent was not comfortable with their own sexuality, or withdrew when concerned about being attracted to their child. Perhaps their parent responded favorably when their child displayed correct behavior, but withdrew if they displayed incorrect behavior. Perhaps the child's request for attention was often rejected by the parent as being a bother if the parent was busy doing something else. Perhaps their parent consistently frowned if their child colored outside the lines or used the wrong color. Perhaps there was a codependent abuse where their parent couldn't take care of themselves, and the child grew up too fast, having to take care of their parent. In any case, this defense lives with a deep-seeded fear of being wrong and unacceptable and that expressing authentic feelings is somehow shameful.

Practice #3: Mending VS. Defending

What Adult Dramas Does This Defense Produce?

This defense breeds adults who have a façade built over their real self, a shield they project to the outside world. They have so long ago sacrificed their authenticity for outward appearance and the pretense of perfection, that they are no longer in touch with their authentic self, rarely aware that it is even missing. Held deeply inside, they combat self-doubt, self-criticism, and insecurity, thinking *"I'm going to fail, not get it right, then no one is going to like me."*

They have a strong need for organizing and planning to perfection, down to the details, and have little patience for imperfection. They want to get it right, and do it better. You will notice their drawers and cupboards are neatly organized, and the clothes in their closet are coordinated and all facing in the same direction.

Since they have high expectations of the world around them that often fails to meet their standards of perfection, they can be annoyed and judgmental with others they see as imperfect. It's common for them to think that if people would *"just do it my way, the right way, then everything would work better"*. Since they come from a place of being all-knowing and completely right, the words they use can come across as critical and make others feel imposed upon, with little room for expanded viewpoints.

They can be pessimistic about people and events in general.

They have a need to be in control and know what is expected and what the next step is. If they perceive the leadership of a group is not producing good results, they will either overtly take charge or covertly maneuver themselves into a place of control.

They are tightly strung and tend towards all or nothing, black and white thinking. They develop rigid habits and rigid ideas about what is "universally" right or wrong.

They can be rejecting, coming from an *"I'll reject you before you reject me"* mindset. When they do, they will cut off or cut out

111

someone who makes them mad or say something to alienate the offender. They can be slow to forgive, and will often hold grudges.

They spend most of their day keeping their mind busy with projects and tasks. They generally shy away from idleness until they are too tired to reflect on their internal critic's negative impact on the people around them.

They externalize their problems. They will point out with a matter-of-fact attitude that they are not the one that made the mistake. If they do accept that they made an error, they judge themselves as a failure. Since their need for perfection is linked to their need for acceptance, it takes a lot of personal growth for them to see themselves as wrong.

When triggered, they maintain a surface of self-sufficiency and not being vulnerable. They will be steely, unemotional, hidden from their own vulnerability. If an unwanted feeling were to come out during a tense situation, they would ask themselves if it were appropriate, and then have a tendency to dissociate from it and want to put it back.

When tensions arise, this defense is good at remaining matter-of-fact. "Never *let them see you sweat*" is their motto. They are capable of holding their emotions tightly inside, and maintaining a poker face. They are often smug during an argument, pointing out their superiority over your emotional response.

They bypass their feelings as feelings are unwieldy and something that needs to be controlled. So they approach life from a mental perspective. Everything is fine with them. People who expose how they are feeling could be a puzzle to them, and are often labeled *drama queens*.

They feel superior but generally don't thrust it on anyone because it's just obvious, of course.

Being tightly clenched, they are often characterized as a tight-ass in the media.

They use sex to obtain approval. It's not difficult for them to have sex without love or love without sex. It's more difficult for them to put the two together. They may even be promiscuous, but without heart, scared to unify the two.

What Are Best Practices For Managing This Defense?

What these adults need most is unconditional acceptance of their imperfection. Whenever the door is open, encourage your partner to notice the many ways that happiness fills other people's lives in ways that are not within your partner's beliefs.

If the stoic, rule abiding, all knowing critic shows up in your partner, and imposes on you their perfect answer, a good response is to ask them to evaluate it in contrast to a higher value. For example, if they are fussing over unnecessary details, try saying to them, *"I understand that you want to do things perfectly. But what is the higher value here: is it doing it perfectly or getting the task done?"* If they are fussing over their high standards for their relationship, try saying to them, *"I understand you want a perfect relationship with a perfect partner. But what is the higher value here: is it having a perfect relationship or is it having someone who loves you?"*

Speak your own truth, but eliminate confrontation. You could do this by finding something you can agree with first, and then add how you disagree. For example, *"Yes, I can see how you heard that, and I heard ... "* or *"Yes, in your shoes, I would feel the same, and in my world, I feel ... "* Notice I used the connective word *"and"* instead of the more common connective word *"but"*. The use of the word *"but"* would have given your listener an inner sense of being negated rather than heard. You want your partner to sense that you are *adding* to the conversation, not *countering* what they have said.

Emphasize the positive versus criticism. They respond best to a constructive approach. For example, change *"I wish you wouldn't do ..."* to *"I always love it when you do ..."*

Give gifts that are either practical or are exquisite in some way.

The higher the chaos, the easier it is for this defense to be calm. Structure, like lists and routines, helps them to prevent overload from chaos. Obtaining a chaotic job that needs their calm, can give them an outlet to excel in other people's eyes.

What Are Some Of The Gifts Born From This Wound?

Integrity
Clarity
Prepared, excels at planning, structure, and organization
Self-reliant
Competent, knows what needs to be done and how
Can dedicate themselves to mastering a craft
Wants to get it right, do an excellent job
Capable of doing many things well
Attention to detail, I's dotted and T's crossed
Matches, lines up and tends to things properly
Neat and well coordinated in their space and dress
Productive, gets things done
Dependable, reliable
Charming and good at small talk
Good etiquette
A love of beauty
Balanced with an exquisite attention to boundaries
Handles situations calmly
Thinks before they speak
Independent

CHAPTER 32
I GET IT!

What I want for you to grasp in this third section is that the underlying cause of most of your unresolved fighting with your partner is that you were bruised as kids, you created some defenses, and now those defenses interfere with your ability to communicate with each other. When that happens, you end up talking to the wall and not to the loving partner safely snuggled behind their wall. And doesn't blaming, shaming and judging only increase the vulnerability this wall is protecting, so the fight becomes unsolvable, resulting in frustration?

When an argument arises, you have a choice now, to say, *"I get it. There's something being triggered here that is hidden behind the curtain of this scene."* Do you want to explore what is behind the curtain? If yes, great; you have the data in this section to help you. If no, that's ok too. But now, you have another choice, haven't you? You can be aware, not take an attack personally, and respond with a more conscious response. When you respond with a response that matches the need that the trigger provoked, notice how compassionate understanding and helpful curiosity replaces confusion and frustration. Can you see how this, in turn, would de-escalate an argument into a more peaceful result? With practice, you will eventually notice fewer and fewer arguments over time as this settles into your automatic behavior. And isn't that priceless!

CHAPTER 33
MENDING VS DEFENDING

Here is a quickie, simplified chart of the most important, key factors for each of the 5 defenses:

Everyone has gone through the 5 stages of development. So everyone has been exposed to the traumas of each stage of growth to a minor or to a major degree.

The Need to Be Connected suffered from some sort of birth trauma.
The Need to Be Nurtured suffered from not being allowed enough.
The Need for Self-Direction suffered from being invaded through over-protection.
The Need for Trust suffered from being invaded through dominance.
The Need for Acceptance suffered from having their affections ignored, refused or embarrassed.

These traumas generated a feeling of shame and being wrong.

The Need to Be Connected felt wrong about being on the planet.
The Need to Be Nurtured felt wrong about having needs.
The Need for Self-Direction felt wrong about saying no.
The Need for Trust felt wrong about being vulnerable.
The Need for Acceptance felt wrong about having feelings.

Feeling wrong generated a sense of insecurity that needed to be defended. Defenses were developed which were later carried into adulthood. Everyone has all 5 defenses. Yet, one tends to dominate more than the others.

Practice #3: Mending VS. Defending

The Need to Be Connected defended by disconnecting, leaving their body for the mental and/or spiritual realms.

The Need to Be Nurtured defended by collapsing, giving up and forgetting their needs.

The Need for Self-Direction defended by retreating into an internal world they made up where no one could touch them.

The Need for Trust defended by conquering through bullying or seduction.

The Need for Acceptance defended by tightening the rules, perfecting their world, and judging how to respond appropriately.

Each defense has at least one key response that helps de-escalate it quickly.

The Need to Be Connected can be quickly helped by grounding and good eye contact.

The Need to Be Nurtured can be quickly helped by bringing them through their feelings, their needs and then asking them to make a request.

The Need for Self-Direction can be helped quickly by giving them choices and asking permission.

The Need for Trust can be helped quickly by meeting them with equal force, assuring them of your loyalty, and then cutting communication until their emotion dissipates.

The Need for Acceptance can be helped quickly by asking them to identify a higher value.

IN SUMMARY

In Summary

CHAPTER 34
PUTTING IT ALL TOGETHER

By changing your perspective on relationship *problems* to relationship *symptoms*, you narrow your choice of solutions. By moving deeper into root causes, can you see how this shrinks the amount of problems you need to solve? By having fewer problems to solve, can you see how much less effort is needed to execute? And less effort means less time and quicker results. So then, with less time, happiness is right around the corner – as soon as you decide to take charge today.

When you choose to solve symptoms instead of root problems, isn't that like taking a pill to cover up a pain? It mellows out for a while – until the next flare up, and then you have to deal with it all over again, right? Or it shows up as a different symptom. But take the time to solve the root cause of the pain, and the symptom goes away permanently, leaving you in peace to enjoy a more vibrant life. Therefore, isn't it better for you to work from the inside out, and fix the cause, than to work from the outside in and fix the symptom? So let me ask you: if you just focused your efforts on only the 3 communication practices you discovered in this small book, even if you let everything else go, how could it not be possible to see a change in the outward symptoms of your relationship? Does anyone really need a PhD to understand what is mere common sense?

Underlying each of the 3 practices you are being encouraged to act on, there is really only

one main skill, the art of communication.

By applying this art to just 3 practices, you laser-focus your efforts, and thus simplify your ability to take charge and create what you want. With YOU in charge, with the skills you discovered here, you can keep that new relationship sizzle with any compatible partner for as long as you desire.

Just like going to the gym and building your body, the more often you exercise these 3 practices, the more you are going to like what you see when you come home each day. Each time you practice, you build that communication muscle – until one day, you realize you are a master.

So be kind to yourself. It has taken you a lifetime to feed poor communication habits into your subconscious. Gift yourself some patience for releasing those old junk communication habits you learned from generations gone by, and some time for replacing those with better, more conscious, healthier habits.

With the control in your hands, or should I say your mouth, you can *take charge and build* a relationship with anyone that you believe fits your values and would make a good friend. Never again will you need to worry that your new-found love may one day end. How soothing is that!

The cornerstone of learning to speak to your partner in such a way, that builds their desire to keep you in their life, is to understand their values and to understand your own. Are you remembering how Dr. John Demartini shared with us that the only thing you can reasonably count on in your relationship is that each person will act according to their own highest values? So each of you discovering each other's values is what will allow each of you to

- fill up your love tanks,
- get your needs met with an unreserved yes
- and end fighting over unresolved traumas.

Taking this down into more detail,

In Summary

- Discovering how to speak each other's highest love value will make you both *feel* loved not just *be* loved. This one daily practice will keep petty annoyances from eroding away the joy and the excitement you felt when you first met.
- Discovering how to ask for your need to be met by linking it to a value your partner treasures, will reward you both with an unreserved yes. When you no longer ask each other to sacrifice one's needs for the other's needs, the opportunity for resentment to drive a wedge into your love bond disappears.
- Discovering how to understand the wall each of you hides behind (to protect the value you place on your vulnerability) will replace unresolved fighting with curiosity and compassion. The old pattern of frustration, blaming and shaming can then be replaced with useful responses that deactivate triggers and de-escalate hurt feelings.

When peace is a staple in your relationship, your needs are being met happily, and your love tank feels full, how eager will you be to meet up with your partner – even after years of being together? Think about it! Success doesn't need to be rocket science.

Hope puts luck in control. But the right knowledge puts YOU into control. With the knowledge of these 3 daily practices, you can create a relationship that you will love being in love with. Getting rid of old ideas that have never worked and building relationships on better ideas that do work will keep your loving bond long after the honeymoon stage is over. So when you are ready to take cause, and stop hoping to stumble into the right relationship, know that there is a better way. You have the option to build your own relationship that is just right for you! Anyone can do it. You can do it!

CHAPTER 35
PRACTICE MAKES PROGRESS

Next steps? Be patient with yourself. Practice makes progress.

Luke Skywalker did not become a Jedi Knight overnight. Great athletes make it to the Olympics by getting up each time they fall. Babies learn to walk by taking the first step, laughing when they land on their butt, and by determining to get it more right the next try.

As you practice the 3 practices for building relationships you strongly want to come home to, the responses you get will immediately begin to change. As you better and better mold them to your own personality, the richer and richer your life will become. Eventually, you will reach for the gold – perfect relationships that give you joy – even within their issues and problems.

In Summary

CHAPTER 36
MASTERY

Napoleon Hill, the famous author of *Think And Grow Rich*, stated that successful goal results were based on:
- a strong *desire* to change your life,
- a *belief* that it is possible,
- *best practices* for making it work,
- *determination* to execute,
- and *persistence* to get it right

(along with 7 other traits). Although written in the 1930's, his formula is still discussed today. Yet, when I read it, he really had my attention – until he got to the 4th and then the 5th and then the 12th practice I had to add in order to achieve an abundant life.

How about simplifying 12 factors into just 3 root factors:
- *clear* about how to accomplish
- *capable* of executing, and
- *motivated* to move forward.

How much easier does that feel? These are the truly important criteria necessary to incorporate any important change in your life. And **what could be more motivating in your life than knowing you can secure and maintain the sizzle and love in that special relationship you found?**

It has been said that *you can't do it wrong, but you can sure do it long*. This means that no matter what path you take to get where you want to go, at least you're moving forward. But some paths take a whole lot longer than others. Doing it yourself requires a certain amount of trial and error to develop the clarity and capability needed to be excellent. However, I have found that a coach or a mentor is the quickest way to gain mastery. After reading this book, you now have the clarity you need to *simplify* the task of *creating* loving relationships by focusing on just three practices daily. If you want to speed up your capability and cut down your practice time even further, I invite you to do it with a coach.

Why is that? Because two heads are better than one. A coach can help you clarify how to apply what you are learning to *your specific situation*. A coach can help you get motivated when you get into a slump. A coach has tools that make you more capable by freeing you from your resistances when a part of you tries to sabotage or roadblock your efforts. A coach can help you practice and give you exercises to deepen your understanding and your ability.

It takes time and motivation to change a lifetime of poor relationship habits. This is your life, and the only one you have right now. Do you want to make the most of the time you have left or flip through a few more unsuccessful years? Is there anything more valuable in the world of happiness than good relationships? Would you really want to put off until tomorrow what you could accomplish today? When you are at the end, looking back on your life, what is going to matter the most? All the hours you put into work? All the hours you spent on hobbies? Or is it going to be the smiles, the love? The work and the hobbies won't go away, but why not do them in an environment of love? So as you get clear on what it takes to create a relationship you love to be in, master it quickly to make the most of the time left. A coach is your best option to speed up that process.

Then as you grow your talent for creating, gently pat yourself on the heart each time you get the result of your focus and time spent reinforcing these new habits. Then celebrate the feedback *YOU created*. YOU did it! You took charge, and YOU made it happen! What is more precious than that!

The Beginning …
and welcome to the start of your journey!

In Summary

THE TOP 5 BOOKS
I LOVED AND RECOMMEND
TO FURTHER YOUR UNDERSTANDING

The 5 Love Languages by Gary Chapman

The Heart Of Love by Dr. John Demartini

Nonviolent Communication by Marshall Rosenberg

How To Win Friends and Influence People by Dale Carnegie

A Course In Miracles by The Foundation For Inner Peace

ABOUT THE AUTHOR

After an excruciatingly painful relationship failure of my own, that left me clawing my way up a 45-degree mountain to feel better, I knew there had to be a better way than just hoping to stumble upon a perfect partner. That's when I went on the quest to solve relationship failure once and for all. Not only for myself, but for all us broken hearted people who think the only safe way to live is by putting our hearts in the freezer.

I've had an instinct for simplifying and problem solving my whole life. So I succeeded in coming up with a simplified solution that could attract everyone's attention. With just 3 (yes, only 3) BEST PRACTICES in communication, I discovered ANYONE could keep their new relationship sizzle glowing long after their honeymoon stage was over. It just takes the RIGHT knowledge, a little willingness to play with the ideas, have FUN with them, and practice practice practice.

During that same period, I looked down my own time line, to the very end, and realized I was not living a life of purpose, only a life of security and success by other people's standards. I had been working the last 24 years as a Senior VP of Finance for a company that taught heart selling, with a focus on embedding behavior for successful change. Yet as I looked at the end of my time line, I knew I didn't want to be one of those statistics that said, *"I wished I had led a life true to myself."* I enjoyed finance, but my passion was peace and relationship building, and I had spent much time at my job helping my team with theirs. So for the next 6 years, I earned certificates in multiple disciplines, so I could apply my passion outside the corporate world and into a life of purpose.

I am now Cheryl Herbst, Hypnotherapist, Energy Healer, Counselor, Life Coach, NLP Master, author, podcaster and most of all, heart mender.

I am currently teaching my simplified XO solution and have my own personal practice helping individuals just like you know that successful relationships aren't so mysterious after all.

What a gift it would be to me to hear your story.

Please share. Here is my email address:
Cheryl@AfraidToLoveAgain.com

I believe it comes down to this: there are many ways to express the same communication. Why not pick the one that gets you the feedback you want? If you have the techniques and skill to work *with* a partner, manipulating and fighting can be thrown into the trash. With the right communication skills, you can stop being a victim to unconscious responses. Instead, you can take charge and *create* the relationship you yearn for. And when you are in charge, *you* diminish the risk of your relationship failures. And when the risk is low, vulnerability feels safe to bloom again. Then you don't have to be

- afraid to love again,
- or afraid of wasting your time,
- or afraid of losing your family and assets,
- or afraid of losing your new-relationship sizzle to apathy.

YOU can have control! And therefore, you can CREATE a relationship you love so you don't have to hope you can stumble into a loving relationship! When you fall in love, the world becomes a happier place. And that benefits everyone!

That is my deepest desire for you!

As a way of saying THANK YOU for your purchase, I would like to gift you a 30-minute consultation as a great way to stay in touch.

To get your **FREE GIFT**,
visit my website at

AfraidToLoveAgain.com

To find out more about how I am helping people like you to rediscover trust, and to take your relationship to new heights of success, tune into my podcast:

X's & O's Not Exes & Woes

In this podcast, I also unfold the 3 practices from this book that keep that new-relationship sizzle glowing long after the honeymoon stage. Additionally, I bring to you stories and interviews of people with real problems just like yours. So tune in, rate and review on iTunes or your favorite channel, and let's make the world a happier, more playful place for everyone!

www.ingramcontent.com/pod-product-compliance
Lightning Source LLC
Chambersburg PA
CBHW071549040426
42452CB00008B/1123